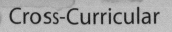

Talk, Thinking and Philosophy in the Primary Classroom

Talk, Thinking and Philosophy in the Primary Classroom

John Smith

LearningMatters

First published in 2010 by Learning Matters Ltd

British Library Cataloguing in Publication Data
A CIP record for this book is available from the British Library.

ISBN 978 1 84445 297 2

This book is also available in the following ebook formats:
Adobe ebook ISBN: 9781844456871
EPUB ebook: ISBN: 9781844456864
Kindle ISBN: 9781844459841

Cover design by Topics – The Creative Partnership
Text design by Code 5 Design Associates
Project management by Deer Park Productions, Tavistock, Devon
Typeset by PDQ Typesetting Ltd, Staffordshire
Printed and bound in Great Britain by Bell & Bain Ltd, Glasgow

Learning Matters Ltd
33 Southernhay East
Exeter EX1 1NX
Tel: 01392 215560
info@learningmatters.co.uk
www.learningmatters.co.uk

Contents

About the author

John Smith is a Senior Lecturer in Primary Education at the Manchester Metropolitan University Institute of Education where he teaches Mathematics Education and Thinking Skills on ITE and CPD courses. He began his teaching career as a teacher of English and communication skills to adults·before moving into primary education. For many years he was a class teacher and subject co-ordinator in a primary school before becoming a teacher educator. John is a Sapere Philosophy for Children trainer and he has also been trained in some of the other approaches described within this book.

Preface

To say that a book represents its author's journey is something of a cliché but it is none-theless a very useful metaphor to describe the process which has led to the publication of this book. The journey in my case has involved a persistent interest in how ideas in our minds are formed, shaped and shared through language. I first encountered these questions while majoring in philosophy as an undergraduate and they have constantly re-emerged in more practical forms over more than three decades of teaching children and adults. There are few questions more important for primary teachers to consider, since the job requires us to help children develop their ideas through the process we call 'learning'. Yet we often devote far more time and energy to the question of what children are to learn, rather than how this astonishing process takes place and the ways that we can best encourage it. In this book we will not ignore the 'what' questions but we will be far more concerned with how these processes occur and the ways we can best assist them.

Experts from many fields, such as psychology, linguistics, neuroscience, cognitive science and philosophy, are also concerned with these issues. It is almost as though teachers and experts from these varied groups are engaged in a tunnel-building project to link the sepa-rate islands on which they are currently located. Eventually, we hope that these tunnels will connect together to form a network which will allow discoveries to flow freely back and forth between classroom, clinic, laboratory and lecture theatre. Such a network is still at an early stage of development but this book will help you to understand some of the most useful ideas for classroom teachers which have emerged to date.

The book is also part of a movement to try to encourage more 'talk' of the kind that stimulates thinking in primary classrooms. The reasons for this will be explored in the chapters to come but, if you are a trainee teacher, you are ideally placed to develop a different kind of approach to that which exists in many classrooms. This different approach is in line with major curriculum changes that are currently taking place and will be boosted enormously by the development of thinking and philosophy in your classroom. You will see that talk, thinking and philosophy support one another and can provide great benefits to the children you teach, helping them develop into the confident, caring and independent lear-ners that every teacher, and parent, wishes to see their children become.

Acknowledgements

I am enormously grateful to many people who have helped me, directly or indirectly, to write this book. Many of my colleagues at the Manchester Metropolitan University Institute of Education have shared their subject expertise generously with me, including Chris Chambers, Ben Steel, Dave Heywood and Duncan Silcock. Particularly large thanks are due to the following colleagues who have given extremely helpful feedback on particular chapters: Yvonne Barnes on Chapters 1 and 2; Dr Gee Macrory on Chapters 3 and 5 and parts of Chapter 7; Dr Gerald Lombard on Chapter 4; Roger Sutcliffe, President of Sapere, on Chapter 6 and part of Chapter 8; Frank Eade and Stuart Naylor on Chapter 7; and David How on Chapter 8. Their collective good counsel has led to many improvements in the book but I must take responsibility for its remaining shortcomings.

I am very grateful to Andrew Willmoth and Ken Jones for their generous help and for their permission to use the TASC wheel in Chapter 6, and to Stuart Naylor and Brenda Keogh of Millgate House Education for their kind permission to use the concept cartoon in Chapter 7. I am grateful to Elizabeth Swaffield who gave permission to use the quotation from Flora Thompson's *Lark Rise*. I am also grateful to many colleagues in Sapere, to Gavin Clowes from Teacher to Teacher UK and to Nigel Newman from the Edward de Bono Foundation UK.

The assistance of colleagues in schools has been invaluable in rooting this book in good practice. My particular thanks go to Head Teacher David How and Barbara Knight from Beaver Road Primary School in Manchester, Head Teacher Simon Beswick from Lime Tree Primary School in Sale, Paula Hammond from Kingsmead Primary School in Northwich and to many other children and staff in those schools. I am also grateful to many students and children I have taught over the years and who have constantly demonstrated that teacher and learner are reversible roles. Thanks are due too to Julia and Amy at Learning Matters and to Jennifer for all of their support and guidance and also to my family and friends for their patience and encouragement during the writing of this book, none more so than my wife Cath and my son David.

I have drawn upon a large number of sources in bringing together the strands of this book and I have tried to credit the originators of every idea and activity I have mentioned. If I have inadvertently failed to attribute credit accurately at any point, then I offer my sincere apologies and, if any such errors are brought to their attention, the publishers will make appropriate adjustments when the book is reprinted.

1
Introduction

Chapter objectives

By the end of this chapter you will have begun to appreciate:

- **how much better your own teaching can become as you develop your professional skills and understanding in talk, thinking and philosophy;**
- **the importance of these skills in the new primary curriculum.**

This will help you to make progress towards these Professional Standards for the award of QTS: **Q1, Q3a, Q15, Q19**

The importance of talking and thinking in the primary classroom

> One year the Inspector, observing a small boy sitting bolt upright gazing before him, called savagely: 'Why are you not writing – you at the end of the row? You have your pen and paper have you not?'
>
>   'Yes, thank you sir.'
>
>   'Then why are you idling?'
>
>   'Please sir, I was only thinking what to say.'
>
> A grunt was the only answer. What other was possible from one who must have known well that pen, ink, and paper were no good without at least a little thinking.
>
> (Thompson, 1939, p190)

As this quotation from Flora Thompson's novel suggests, thinking can easily be confused with idleness. Perhaps the most telling sentence is the last one. How could anyone seriously believe that the simple act of using a pen or even, in our own times, the most sophisticated word processor could lead to a worthwhile outcome without some thinking on the part of its user. Yet thinking is very easy to overlook, even for teachers. The constant flow of thought through our minds is well described by Steve Bowkett:

> Thoughts stream through our minds all day long, often without us paying much attention to them. Even when we do notice what's 'on our mind' we might take this mental material quite for granted or, alas, forget most of it without considering how it can be used to our greatest benefit.
>
> (Bowkett, 2007, pxiii)

So how can we fail to notice something of such vital importance? When we drive a car we are generally unaware of the workings of the engine. Similarly, every reader of this book knows that children are thinking constantly and could easily recognise the accuracy of Steve Bowkett's description. Like the busy driver, however, teachers are caught up in what they do – the very demanding business of classroom teaching. They often forget the importance of thinking and imagine, as the school inspector seems to have done, that what is written down or recorded in some other way is all that matters. If we make this error, another error follows on from it quite naturally: the idea that no serious attention needs to be paid, by teacher or child, to the process of thinking. This book will help you to challenge that notion. In the process of challenging it, you will find it easier to meet the Standards for Teaching and you will become a better teacher.

The next time you undertake a piece of written work – a lesson evaluation or course assignment for example – try to capture some of your thought processes as you prepare to write it. You could jot down some notes or draw a diagram to try and represent this. How does one thought lead to another? You will not be able to capture much of this: there are too many strands to our thinking and our thoughts are elusive and rapidly changing. A brief attempt though should be enough to prove just how complex and diverse your thinking is, just like that of your children.

As far as classroom talk goes, there is a similar picture. Although every teacher is aware of its importance, evidence strongly suggests that classrooms often fail to provide children with the opportunities that they need to talk in ways which best support learning. There is of course a need for order to be maintained within your classroom and therefore to encourage children to talk as much as they want, at all times, is not necessarily the best approach for you to take. As you work your way through this book you will develop achievable strategies for encouraging the kind of talk which is purposeful and which allows for the development of thinking. Better still, you will develop the ability to help children to recognise and regulate such talk themselves.

An exciting time to develop talk, thinking and philosophy

How can we set up the conditions for such productive talking and thinking to emerge in our classrooms? There is a range of approaches which will be examined in this book. One approach which will be discussed a great deal is Philosophy for Children (P4C). As the name suggests, P4C is a classroom approach which has strong roots in philosophy and which helps children develop their skills in talk, in thinking and in other important areas too such as 'emotional intelligence', which will be considered in Chapter 4. You may still wonder why it is important to invest any time or effort into these areas. Can the teacher have any influence over the development of children's talk and thinking or will they just happen by themselves if we get on with our teaching? The bad news is that if we ignore them we are likely to offer children inadequate opportunities for development. The good news is that there are tried and tested ways of encouraging them and some of these are quite straightforward. Others require more investment in terms of time and energy but the benefits they offer will easily repay this investment. To give you a clearer idea of some possible directions that you may eventually travel in as you work through this book, consider the following three Classroom Stories. They are composite pictures but, like all of the Classroom and School Stories in this book, they are based upon real trainee and teacher experiences.

CLASSROOM STORY 1

Amy has decided that she would like to help the Year 5 children in her placement class to develop their talking and thinking in her science lessons. She has obtained a book of concept cartoons (Naylor and Keogh, 2000) and she asks the children to discuss their ideas about light and dark using the example shown in Chapter 7. She notices how the opinions aired in the cartoon act as a stimulus for the children in her class to explore their own ideas about this area of science. The device of considering other children's ideas about the topic seems to 'unlock' her children's beliefs and misconceptions.

CLASSROOM STORY 2

Ben has read about P4C and has also heard a colleague in school speaking enthusiastically about it, following a training course she has attended. Ben has decided to run a 'community of enquiry', the core practice of P4C, with his Year 1 class. Using the book *But Why?* (Stanley, 2004) for guidance, he decides to use the children's book *If I were a spider* (Bowkett, 2004) as the stimulus for an enquiry. He is astonished by the quality of questions the children in his class generate themselves and then attempt to answer. He decides that he will continue leading enquiries in his class and try to undertake training as soon as possible to develop his understanding further.

CLASSROOM STORY 3

A school which takes many trainee teachers on their placements has implemented a range of approaches to the development of thinking skills. In particular, the school uses Thinking Actively in a Social Context or TASC, an approach devised by Belle Wallace and collaborators (see, for example, Wallace, 2002) alongside Edward de Bono's *Six Thinking Hats* (de Bono, 1985). Trainees have valuable opportunities to witness the development of children's thinking skills as they move through the school. They notice that children seem able to produce many creative responses when they are faced with problem-solving situations. They also notice how confident and self-reliant the children seem to be and how well they evaluate their own learning.

As you read through these classroom stories you will probably have noticed that some changes in your practice – like the use of concept cartoons in Classroom Story 1 – can be put into place very easily. You could introduce such changes within a matter of days. Other changes, like the introduction of P4C in Classroom Story 2, require more preparation but you could make a start in your own classroom quite soon. This book will explain the rationale and basic practices of these and other approaches to talk, thinking and philosophy. It will also help you to understand some of the important background issues which underpin classroom work of this kind and it will point you in the direction of further reading and training which will be essential if you wish to continue developing your practice in these areas. If you are lucky enough to be placed at a school like the one in Classroom Story 3, this book will enable you to take advantage of what it has to offer and, after you have qualified, to contribute to similar development in the schools in which you work. This is a project that could last for your whole career in teaching.

How can this book help you to develop?

If you are a trainee teacher you will find this book particularly useful as it has been written primarily with your needs in mind, along with the other books in the Learning Matters *Achieving QTS* series, particularly the *Cross Curricular Strand* series to which it belongs. However, given the diversity of teacher training routes currently available, the circumstances in which training is undertaken will vary greatly from one reader to another. This book will refer both to your own classroom situation and to a wider picture of national and international research. Whatever the circumstances of your training, therefore, you will be able to develop your own knowledge and understanding of the issues covered, as well as the skill and confidence needed to try out some of the ideas described here in your own classroom. The book is intended to equip you with a 'survival kit' to get you started on a mission to create the best possible conditions for talk, thinking and philosophy in your classroom, which in turn will create the best possible conditions for teaching and learning across the curriculum. Within the book you will encounter ideas that you may meet in the taught elements of your teacher training programme. The book will support and extend such work but it can also be used for independent study if you do not have access to such elements in a taught programme.

This book should also be useful to newly qualified and experienced teachers because, once you have acquired the survival kit required by the trainee teacher, the issues raised will continue to pose challenges for you as a more experienced teacher. All good teachers work hard to develop their existing practice and there are few areas more fruitful to develop than those covered by this book. As a more experienced teacher, you might also be looking beyond your own classroom and considering ways in which whole-school change might be brought about so that you can help make your school one in which talk, thinking and philosophy are celebrated as vital activities. Chapter 8 offers some guidance about how to help your school develop into a Thinking School.

This book will build up a case for collaborative work in the classroom in which ideas can be exchanged through talk. In the same spirit, you are recommended to try to work collaboratively with others as you study the book. It can certainly be studied alone but you are likely to reap even greater benefit through discussion with others about the issues raised. The Professional Standards at 'Q' level relating to the topics covered are listed at the beginning of each chapter.

There are already many excellent books about talking, thinking and philosophy in the primary classroom. Some link the three as this book does although many others deal with just one or two of these three areas. Reference will be made to some of these books in the chapters to come. This book, though, tackles all three of these interrelated areas from the point of view of the trainee teacher. Quite a number of other books examine one particular approach to the development of talking or thinking, such as TASC or P4C, and one of the purposes of this book is to draw some of these approaches together so that you can see the similarities and differences between them. I will repeatedly remind you that no single approach is likely to meet all of your children's needs. By considering a variety of approaches, therefore, as you will in the chapters that follow, you will be able to make an informed choice about some approaches which you might follow in your own classroom.

How is this book organised?

The issues addressed by this book are timeless ones which successive generations of teachers have attempted to deal with but those teachers have not always been as well supported by the prevailing ideas of their times as current teachers are. Many schools are using the new primary curriculum which was introduced by the Labour government in early 2010 and Chapters 6 and 7 show how well this curriculum supports talk, thinking and philosophy. No matter what form the primary curriculum eventually takes however, it will be vital to include these three elements. With each passing year we also get a clearer picture from neuroscience about the conditions which affect thinking and learning and these insights, which we will examine in this book, can help you to teach more effectively.

The chapters are sequential and will cross-reference one another but you can read them in your own preferred order if you wish. Chapter 2 examines the reasons why we should teach talk, thinking and philosophy. Chapters 3 and 4 deal with important background theory related to these areas and, unless you already have a very good background knowledge of these issues, you are recommended to read these chapters before the later ones. Chapters 5 and 6 examine a range of approaches to talk, thinking and philosophy that you can develop in your classroom. Chapter 7 takes a subject-specific view of these approaches and will help you to teach them in ways which are consistent with current practice and with proposed changes to the primary curriculum. Chapter 8 will consider the ways in which these changes can be reinforced across the school.

PRACTICAL TASK PRACTICAL TASK **PRACTICAL TASK** PRACTICAL TASK **PRACTICAL TASK**

List your main priorities for development (as you currently see them) as you prepare to work your way through this book. It may be helpful to list them according to the chapter structure of the book so that they can serve as an action plan. After you have finished studying each chapter, try to identify at least two personal targets that will help you to develop your practice. Try to make these a mixture of targets that you can achieve quickly and targets that will take longer to fully reach.

A SUMMARY OF **KEY POINTS**

> Developing your ability to teach talk, thinking and philosophy will help you to improve your teaching skills and will benefit the children in your class. These are vital parts of the primary curriculum. They can also be great fun for teachers and children.

> The present time is a particularly good one for developing these skills because of the major curriculum changes which are taking place and because of our growing understanding of how children learn.

REFERENCES REFERENCES **REFERENCES** REFERENCES **REFERENCES** REFERENCES

Bowkett, S (2004) *If I were a spider.* Stafford: Network Educational Press.

Bowkett, S (2007) *100+ ideas for teaching thinking skills.* London: Continuum.

de Bono, E (1985) *Six thinking hats.* London: Penguin Books.

Naylor, S and Keogh, B (2000) *Concept cartoons in science education.* Sandbach: Millgate House Publishers.

Stanley, S (2004) *But why?* Stafford: Network Educational Press.

Thompson, F (1939) *Lark Rise.* Oxford: Oxford University Press.

Wallace, B (2002) *Teaching thinking skills across the early years.* London: David Fulton Publishers.

Useful websites

The following link takes you to the new primary curriculum:

www.curriculum.qcda.gov.uk/new-primary-curriculum. This will be an extremely useful reference point throughout this book.

The Professional Standards can be accessed in full at

www.tda.gov.uk/teachers/professionalstandards

2
Why teach talk, thinking and philosophy?

Chapter objectives

By the end of this chapter you will have:

- considered the benefits to primary children of developing their talking and thinking skills;
- begun to consider the importance of philosophy in the classroom;
- considered the ways in which work of this kind can help primary children develop their potential as citizens of the future;
- considered the links between these areas and the aims of the new primary curriculum.

This will help you to make progress towards these Professional Standards for the award of QTS: **Q1, Q3a, Q15, Q19**

Introduction: shifting your perspective from product to process

Let us think once again of the school inspector who was put in his place by the simple honesty of the young boy in the extract from Flora Thompson's novel at the beginning of Chapter 1. Whenever we look at a child's work, whether it is a model made from junk materials, a piece of writing or the solutions to a set of mathematical problems, we can look at it from two different perspectives. From the first perspective we can consider the quality of that work as a response to the task set. This is a very important perspective and one which we consider on a daily basis. The second perspective is also of vital importance but it is easily overlooked. It is to consider the child's work as evidence of the thinking which led up to it. This leads us to some extremely interesting insights.

- We can never have direct contact with a child's thinking.
- We can, however, use a range of evidence to build up our understanding of the thinking which has taken place for the child to have accomplished a particular task, or set of tasks. We can also assess how well the child's thinking is developing over time and decide how we can best help this process to continue.

There is a third important point which follows from these two.

- Children's talk will often give a better indication of the quality of their thinking and how it is developing than their writing can.

What you have considered in this section is often described by teachers as focusing on the 'process' of learning rather than the 'product' (an idea first suggested by Jerome Bruner) and it is very important to learn to do this. Of course this is not to say that the 'products' of learning are not worthwhile in themselves, but making the mental switch to focusing on the process, at least for some of the time, is an important skill for a teacher to develop and can result in quite different judgements being made about a child's achievement.

Talking and thinking are hard to separate

The role of talking and social interaction in the development of children's thinking is a crucial issue for you to recognise and one which is central to this book. While talking and thinking could be examined in isolation from one another, you will find it more useful to consider them in combination, since they are inextricably linked. Some time ago I video-taped an interview with a small group of children in a Reception class. I asked the children a number of questions including, 'How big is your house?' (You can read about all of these interviews in Smith, 2008a if you would like to know more). The children, all aged four or five, answered by holding their hands apart and making statements like 'This big' and 'That big'. Some time later, I asked some trainee teachers on a Thinking Skills course the same question. Read the trainees' responses to this question and then try out the Practical Tasks below.

> Trainee A: My house is a three-bedroomed house. It's semi-detached. I would say it's probably medium size. It's got two big gardens front and back. It's got a driveway and a garage... It's just a standard size...

> Trainee B: My house has got four bedrooms. It's got a garden front and back as well. It's got a drive and a garage as well but we've extended ours. It's still average size I'd say, not big...

PRACTICAL TASK PRACTICAL TASK **PRACTICAL TASK** PRACTICAL TASK **PRACTICAL TASK**

First consider the following questions.

- Why might the young children and the trainees have answered the question about their houses in such different ways?
- Could the things they each said tell us anything about what they thought?

Next, try to find the opportunity to discuss 'everyday' questions like this with any young children you are currently working with to see if you get a similar response. If you are working with mixed age groups, note the differences between children of different ages. Do you notice any patterns?

In the next two chapters you will consider some important ideas about how children think and these ideas may make you look at these examples in a different light. First, however, we must consider the most fundamental question within this chapter.

Why should we teach talk, thinking and philosophy?

Why should you bother trying to teach these skills rather than ignoring them and letting them develop of their own accord? There are a range of answers which could be offered to this question. Five of these will be considered below and they highlight the importance of the issues addressed in this book.

1. We should teach them because... talking and thinking underpin most of the learning which takes place in school

A difficulty facing teachers who wish to develop their teaching in this area is the fact that talk happens very often and thinking appears to happen all the time. It seems reasonable to assume therefore that the teacher can do little to influence these two processes, but one of the main purposes of this book is to challenge that assumption. Suggesting that a direct focus on thinking should be a central part of a child's education is not a new idea. A great variety of work in this area of teaching has developed in many countries over the last half century and indeed the origins of such approaches can be traced much further back in time, at least to the influential writing of John Dewey (for example, Dewey, 1910). In 1999 Carol McGuinness led an important governmental review of such initiatives being used in schools in this country (McGuinness, 1999) and, shortly afterwards, thinking skills became established within the version of the National Curriculum which took effect in 2000 (DfEE, 1999).

Edward de Bono, a leading authority on thinking skills, has suggested that they should be treated as a school subject in their own right, to be taught alongside literacy and numeracy. He believes that most schools give insufficient attention to the development of thinking skills and he suggests the name 'operacy' for this new area of the curriculum (de Bono, 1992). Like de Bono, an increasing number of educators feel that thinking skills are not given enough emphasis in the curriculum, although they do not all agree about the content of this area or about whether it should be a separate subject or should instead permeate the existing subjects. Developing these aspects of your own practice will allow you to clarify your views on these questions and to engage professionally with much exciting work that is emerging in schools.

Later chapters of this book, particularly Chapter 6, will make the case for teaching philosophy as an important element of teaching thinking skills. It is sufficient at this point to note that philosophy has a long and honourable tradition in the post-school curriculum and increasingly that heritage is being seen as relevant for students of all ages.

The development of talk in the primary classroom has had a similarly uneven development, as you will see in Chapter 3. The term 'oracy' is often used to describe this aspect of language and, as with the teaching of thinking, many critics suggest that primary teachers have not always been as effective as they could be in helping children to develop their skills in this area (Smith, 2010). An exciting new approach called 'dialogic teaching' has been evolving over the last few years and, as we shall discover, practitioners following its principles are beginning to create and exploit opportunities in which high quality talk and thinking can develop. Based on the work of Robin Alexander (Alexander, 2008) and others, dialogic teaching is one of the most important and innovative movements in primary education today and the pedagogy that it recommends is compatible with many of the approaches considered in this book. Dialogic teaching will be considered in a number of chapters, particularly Chapters 3 and 5.

PRACTICAL TASK PRACTICAL TASK **PRACTICAL TASK** PRACTICAL TASK **PRACTICAL TASK**

Make a list of any strategies you have seen teachers employ to encourage the development of children's talk and thinking such as 'talk partners' or giving children thinking time when questions are asked. Talk to these teachers about what you have observed and try to find out their intentions in employing such strategies. List too any actions of this kind that you have already taken yourself to achieve these objectives. How effective have these been?

2. We should teach them because . . . teaching these skills will help children reach their potential as learners

A quiet revolution has been taking place in the primary curriculum since the turn of the millennium. In the decade or so before, the primary curriculum had developed into one which was, in the main, organised according to its constituent subjects. (More detail of this is given in Chapter 7 and you might also like to read Smith, 2008b for a fuller account of these changes.) A growing number of commentators, from within education and beyond, began to voice their concerns that the primary curriculum, with its rigid subject categories, was not equipping children adequately for the changing world around them. Rather than being so heavily dominated by the subjects within it, critics argued that the primary curriculum should be reorganised so that greater priority could be given to relevant topics, themes and first-hand experiences which would engage children's interest as they learned.

One model for such a holistic and child-centred approach has been the Early Years Foundation Stage curriculum in the UK. Areas of Learning were proposed in the *Final Report of the Rose Review* (DCSF, 2009; referred to from this point as the *Rose Report* and the *Rose Review* for easier reading) and these have been adopted in the new primary curriculum. They are quite close, though not identical, to those in the Early Years Foundation Stage curriculum. Rather than concentrating so heavily on the content areas specified within each subject, it has often been suggested that teachers should work to develop the core skills which underlie the subjects of the curriculum. The *Rose Report* partly adopted this approach and the new primary curriculum has followed in the same direction. It should be noted though that the new primary curriculum is something of a halfway house on this issue, incorporating, as it does, both skills and bodies of knowledge. There are arguments against heavily skills-based curricular models (Alexander, 2006) but once skills are identified, talking and thinking inevitably feature high on any list suggested and they do so in the new primary curriculum. We will explore these issues more fully in Chapters 6, 7 and 8.

Another important change in recent years has been the increased importance attached to helping children to manage and direct their own learning. A phrase which has been around in education for some time and which sums up this intention quite neatly is 'learning to learn'. This phrase has become part of key guidance materials offered to teachers in recent years and one of the aims of the new primary curriculum is that children should be successful learners, a very similar aspiration. Focusing upon learning to learn requires children to consider their own thinking processes, a process called 'metacognition' which you will hear more about in later chapters. Strong evidence that this sort of approach is beneficial to children comes from the results of a major study of the effectiveness of educational interventions upon children's attainment led by Professor John Hattie. Taking account of approximately 50,000 studies from across the English-speaking world over a 15-year period, Hattie has identified the most and least effective interventions in the educational process in terms of their effects upon children's attainment. In this study, teaching strategies to encourage metacognition were found to be particularly effective (Hattie, 2008, pp188–89).

PRACTICAL TASK PRACTICAL TASK **PRACTICAL TASK** PRACTICAL TASK **PRACTICAL TASK**

Ask a teacher in the school where you are currently working if you can observe a lesson in which children will be asked, at some point, to reflect on their own thinking and learning. Good opportunities often arise during the daily mathematics lesson when children explain their methods for solving calculations. How does the teacher encourage this kind of metacognition?

'Personalised learning' is another important notion in current primary practice (see, for example, Wilmot, 2006). Essentially, this suggests that teachers and schools should not provide education on a 'one size fits all' basis but should take account of the individual needs of the children before them. This is a challenging idea – and one which has sometimes led to stronger rhetoric than reality – but it is an important one too and, as I shall discuss in Chapter 8, the development of talking, thinking and philosophical skills can be a key strategy in pursuit of this goal. The growing importance of children's own views about what they are taught and how their schools should be run should be borne in mind here too. This is often referred to as 'pupil voice' and most schools now have structures to encourage children to give their views on all aspects of school life. This issue relates to another aim of the new primary curriculum, that children should become confident individuals and we will revisit it in Chapter 8.

3. We should teach them because . . . it will help children to lead happier and more fulfilled lives as citizens of the future

Placing so much emphasis on learning to learn may seem misguided to some readers. Sceptics might suggest that teachers should spend their time instilling in children those bodies of knowledge which have been handed down from the past but this is a contestable idea. The world which awaits the children currently in our primary schools is certain to be very different to the one that their parents and teachers have grown up in (although it is likely to be similar in many ways too – a point easily overlooked by those predicting the future). Alvin Toffler has famously suggested that the *illiterate of the 21st century will not be those who cannot read and write, but those who cannot learn, unlearn, and relearn* (Gibson, 1998, Foreword).

Many of the children in our primary schools at the time of writing should still be alive in the twenty-second century. All who live beyond the next few decades are likely to see a world coming to terms with the next stages of global warming and the intensification of a range of environmental challenges with both local and global consequences. On a less gloomy but no less challenging note, they are likely to see further breakthroughs in medicine, communications and other technologies which have shifted from science fiction to scientific reality in our own lifetimes, such as genetic engineering, the internet, nanotechnology and robotics. We have already seen extraordinary changes in the ways that children and young people work, play and relate to one another in affluent Western societies compared to the fairly recent past, and talking and thinking play as great a part in these as ever. Children will need ever greater flexibility of thought as they cope with the demands of this rapidly changing world. They will also need creativity to contribute to the solutions which will hopefully emerge to the major challenges facing humankind this century. There will be a need too for greater ethical sensibility as the citizens of tomorrow seek to make appropriate choices in new ethical contexts. To develop this range of cognitive abilities, children will also need to develop the personal qualities which will support their development as learners and as citizens. Guy Claxton has produced important work in this area (for example, Claxton, 2002) which relates strongly to thinking skills and which we will consider in Chapter 6.

Up to this point 'talking and thinking skills' have been treated as though everyone who uses these terms understands them in the same way. This is not the case and in the following chapters you will be helped to understand the different interpretations which key educationalists have made of them. At this point, however, it is important to make clear that the development of these skills should always take place in ways which help children develop as rational and caring beings. Each day the news contains examples of humans behaving in atrocious ways to one another, ways which seem incomprehensible to most people. While there are no easy ways of preventing such actions – and it should certainly not be seen as the responsibility of the school to prevent them – they highlight the need for greater emphasis upon classroom approaches which are designed to encourage rationality and consideration for others in the lives of young people as they develop into the citizens of the future. Various words can be used to describe these attributes but the word 'citizenship' is a useful umbrella term and the new primary curriculum places considerable emphasis on learning in this area, the third of its trio of aims being to develop responsible citizens.

Sadly, we know that some young people will be difficult – and perhaps impossible – for even the most skilled teachers to reach. Some of the most vulnerable children stop attending school at the earliest opportunity anyway. We may, however, make a crucial difference in the lives of many of the children we teach if we adopt such practices and help them to assess their own actions and the actions of others on a more rational basis. Communication is of course a two-way process and Michelle MacGrath stresses the importance of teachers' own communication with children as a key factor in helping to develop behaviour, motivation and co-operation among children (MacGrath, 2000, pp72–9)

One very useful approach which has already been mentioned several times is P4C, which aims to develop children's thinking abilities and, to use a phrase we will expand upon later, their emotional intelligence. As we shall see in Chapter 6, an important feature of P4C is that it aims to help children to become more 'reasonable' in two related senses. They should be able to reason and they should be reasonable in the everyday sense of the word. This distinction is very important to recognise. If we see our task as simply developing children's thinking skills as though we were programming a computer, we may not help them develop ethically, emotionally or in other ways that will allow them to live well as human beings. There are other approaches to reasoned discussion, such as Open Spaces for Dialogue in Education (OSDE), which attempt to help children to respect different cultural perspectives in a world of increasing interdependence. The *Ajegbo Report, Curriculum Review. Diversity and Citizenship*, produced after the London tube bombings, commends both P4C and OSDE and states that a *significant outcome of P4C has been for pupils to develop 'a greater sense of spiritual intelligence' and empathy with their peers. The importance of pupils developing such higher order thinking skills when exploring concepts and processes in education for diversity is a key priority* (DfES, 2007, p47).

REFLECTIVE TASK

Consider the classrooms in which you have learned or had influence as a trainee teacher. To what extent have you and the teachers responsible for those classrooms attempted to appeal to children's rationality (their sense of reason and fairness) and sense of citizenship when helping resolve classroom disputes? Consider too the effects of the ways children are spoken to by the adults looking after them. Do you think that taking these issues into account helps children in the immediate situation and beyond?

4. We should teach them because... they are part of the National Curriculum and children cannot access the curriculum properly without them

You are probably already aware of the importance of talk in the National Curriculum which is contained within the English Attainment Target 'Speaking and Listening' (DfEE, 1999). Trainee teachers often find this area difficult to plan for, however, and many references to Speaking and Listening in their plans often seem 'bolted on' to meet the demands of assessors, rather than playing a vital and integrated part in their teaching. This book can help you to become much clearer about the part played in your teaching by children's talk and therefore to plan activities of real value, particularly as you begin to use the new primary curriculum.

While most primary trainees recognise that talk is an essential part of the primary curriculum, many are unaware that thinking skills have also been part of the National Curriculum for quite some time too. The version which has been in schools during the last decade has a section (DfEE, 1999, p22) in which thinking skills are set out in detail. This has not, however, led to the emphasis on these skills that was hoped for and many teachers and trainee teachers are unaware of these requirements. We will examine the forthcoming changes to the National Curriculum in Chapters 6 and 7.

5. We should teach them because... teaching these skills is likely to make what happens in your classroom more enjoyable

A common effect that occurs when trainee teachers or experienced teachers are introduced to work of this kind is a quantum leap in their job satisfaction levels. Teacher evaluations of the effect of P4C, for example, have often included teacher comments suggesting that this approach has allowed them to teach in the way that they hoped they would when they came into the profession. The principle reason for this kind of reaction seems to be the enormous satisfaction that teachers gain from children's responses to approaches which invite them to be rational, creative and communicative. The effects upon the life of schools can also be profound. Of course it is dangerous to see any single approach, or even a set of approaches, as a panacea for all ills, but children who are given a sense of purpose, pride and fairness in school, who are encouraged to be confident and caring communicators, and who are invited to take a significant part in their own educational journey, are liable to become happy and enthusiastic learners. And you will notice a remarkably strong correlation between happy learners and happy teachers – wherever you find one, the other is usually close by.

A SUMMARY OF **KEY POINTS**

> Although talking and thinking can be examined separately, there is a great deal to be gained by thinking about them alongside one another since they are hard to separate in practice.

> You should try to develop the habit of focusing on the process which has led to a particular piece of work from a child rather than just focusing on the product the child has produced.

> Developing their talking and thinking skills will help children to succeed in school and will help them prepare for their lives as citizens of the future.

REFERENCES REFERENCES **REFERENCES** REFERENCES **REFERENCES** REFERENCES

Alexander, R J (2006) *Education as dialogue. Moral and pedagogical choices for a runaway world.* York: Dialogos.

Alexander, R J (2008) *Towards dialogic teaching.* (4th Edition) York: Dialogos.

Claxton, G (2002) *Building learning power. Helping young people become better learners.* Bristol: TLO Limited.

DCSF (2009) *Independent review of the primary curriculum: Final Report (The Rose Report).* Nottingham: DCFS.

de Bono, E (1992) *Teach your child how to think.* London: Penguin Books.

Dewey, J (1910) *How we think.* Boston: D C Heath and Company.

DfEE (1999) *The National Curriculum: handbook for primary teachers in England.* London: HMSO.

DfES (2007) *Curriculum review. Diversity and citizenship.* Nottingham: DfES Publcations.

Gibson, R (ed) (1998) *Rethinking the future: rethinking business principles, competition, control and complexity, leadership, markets and the world.* (New Edition) London: Nicholas Brealey Publishing Limited.

Hattie, J (2008) *Visible learning. A synthesis of over 800 meta-analyses relating to achievement.* London: Routledge Education.

MacGrath, M (2000) *The art of peaceful teaching in the primary school.* London: David Fulton Publishers.

McGuinness, C (1999) *From thinking skills to thinking classrooms: a review and evaluation of approaches to developing pupils' thinking.* London: DfEE Research Report RR115.

Smith, J (2008a) How big is your house? *Primary Mathematics*, 12(2): 8–10.

Smith, J (2008b) Reconciling subjects and contexts: the case for a pragmatic primary curriculum. *Educational Futures. Journal of the British Education Studies Association Conference Edition*, 1(2): 63–74. Accessible at *www.educationstudies.org.uk/materials/vol_1issue_2_j_smith_final.pdf.*

Smith, J (2010) Speaking up: towards a more oracy-based classroom. *English Drama Media*, 16: 29–33 Sheffield: NATE.

Wilmot, E (2006) *Personalising learning in the primary school.* Carmarthen: Crown House Publishing Ltd.

Useful websites

You can find out more about *P4C* at the SAPERE website at www.sapere.org.uk. You can find out more about TASC at www.tascwheel.com and about Edward de Bono's approaches, including Six Thinking Hats, at www.debonofoundation.co.uk.

3
Talk theory

Chapter objectives

By the end of this chapter you will have considered:

- **how children learn to talk;**
- **how children's talk and thought are connected;**
- **factors which can affect children's talk;**
- **the importance of establishing more productive talk;**
- **the development of 'dialogic teaching' in primary classrooms.**

This will help you to make progress towards these Professional Standards for the award of QTS:
Q1, Q2, Q4, Q6, Q7a, Q8, Q10, Q14, Q18, Q19, Q21b, Q25c, Q29.

Introduction

As you work through this chapter, you will develop your understanding of the crucial relationships between talking and learning. The insights drawn together here are from a wide variety of disciplines such as linguistics, psychology and cognitive science and they include contributions from some major educational thinkers. In order to provide you with a concise and usable introduction to this field there is inevitably some compression of the complex discussion and debate that lies behind the issues raised in this chapter and the one that follows.

All teachers are concerned with the development of children's talk and this chapter and others will help you understand why this is such a key priority. Chapter 5 will build upon the theory outlined in this chapter to provide you with a variety of approaches to try out in the classrooms in which you are working and training. As you study Chapter 3 you will also become aware of the inextricable links which exist between talking and thinking and you will realise that a study of one without the other is of limited use to the teacher, since it is through talk that children's thoughts are formed, shaped and shared. This awareness will develop as you study Chapter 4 which shifts the focus to thinking and philosophy.

Talking among pre-school children

Of all our accomplishments, talking is probably the most remarkable. When we welcome a new baby into our family, we hear no words (although we generally hear a great deal of sound). From the earliest stages of life though, children are using whatever vocal sounds are available to them to communicate and they are trying to make sense of the strange sounds made by those around them. It is astonishing that small children are able to distinguish any elements of language in what they hear. When speech is analysed using a sound spectrogram, the record reveals that breaks between words are often impossible to recognise, the input being instead a continuous stream of sound. Young children must therefore identify the words within the sounds that they hear. They must then make sense of their meaning before babbling themselves (an important stage in preparing to speak) and producing their own first words, usually at around one year of age. From that point onwards, under normal circumstances, children's acquisition and skill in using language proceeds at a remarkable pace. Average vocabulary estimates can be very misleading, since the vocabulary that children speak and understand varies greatly, but research by Fenson *et al.* (cited in Harris, 2004) provides some useful insights into young children's language development. In terms of understanding, they found that, while both boys and girls typically understood only a few dozen words at eight months of age, by 16 months boys understood more than 150 words and girls understood more than 200 words. As you might expect, the number of words spoken by children at 16 months was considerably fewer than the number of words understood, but the gender difference was noticeable here too with girls producing far more than boys (Harris, 2004). Once begun, this remarkable process gathers momentum. By one and a half, children typically begin to combine words and, by two or three, they produce more grammatically sophisticated utterances. By the time they reach normal school age, both boys and girls will generally understand and be able to produce many more words, blended into sentences of considerable complexity. It is worth reminding yourself that no matter how early in their school lives you meet them, all of the children you teach will have had these experiences, in whichever language or languages they have been exposed to.

It must be emphasised once again that the generalised picture given above masks wide variation between individuals and the fact that some children reach a particular milestone before or after their peers will rarely have any lasting significance. Clearly, however, delay or other problems with a child's speech can occasionally be a sign that something more serious is amiss. Although, as a teacher, you cannot have the knowledge and experience of language development that speech therapists or child psychologists possess, it is very useful for you to have some idea of how children's talk develops. While you should guard against leaping to unwarranted conclusions on the basis of this limited knowledge, it is important to recognise that the teacher's role can be very important in the identification of any developmental difficulties a child may have, a point emphasised by the recent *Bercow Report* (DCSF, 2008). If you are concerned by a child's limitations in talking and understanding, discuss your concerns with more experienced colleagues such as your class teacher, the school mentor or the school Special Educational Needs Co-ordinator (SENCO). They will consider a range of evidence and involve the child's parents and other professionals if they believe that the situation merits further investigation. Recent changes in education are designed to ensure that there is more effective communication between teachers and other professionals working with children. If you are working or training in a multi-agency setting, therefore, you may be able to speak directly to a speech therapist or child psychologist but your mentor or class teacher should always be your first point of contact.

How do children learn to talk?

The previous section described, in very broad terms, the development of pre-school children's talking skills but we have not considered the way in which this takes place. There has been a great deal of debate about the process by which children acquire language but, as with a number of other important debates considered in this book, there is still a lack of consensus about precisely how this happens. As part of this study of children's talk, it is useful to consider some of the main models as these will also help you to understand some important underlying ideas about how children think and learn.

Behaviourist models

In the middle of the twentieth century, behaviourist explanations of psychological processes were extremely influential. All such models are based upon the idea that humans learn by responding to stimuli and they include the related idea that rewarding particular behaviours leads to their repetition. You have probably come across the account of Pavlov's dog which would salivate whenever a bell was rung to announce the imminent arrival of food. The most interesting feature of that situation was that, since food regularly appeared at the sound of the bell, the dog's response was reinforced to the point that it would salivate at the sound of the bell, regardless of whether food appeared. Although behaviourists would readily concede that most human learning is far more complex than this, they have suggested that even high-level skills, such as language acquisition, are developed in comparable ways. Behaviourist psychologists, such as B F Skinner (Skinner, 1957), have argued that a young child presented with a stimulus, like the desire for food or a favourite toy, might be provoked to say a word which she had noticed was in some way associated with the desired object, such as 'Apple' or 'Teddy'. Eventually, a more complex set of words such as 'Want apple' or 'Give me teddy' would be produced and the child's language would become richer and closer in form to that of an adult. The rewards obtained (apples, teddies, etc.) would reinforce this language usage. An important feature of this model is that, certainly in the early stages, we do not need to assume any understanding of, for example, the underlying grammar of the language on the part of children as they learn to talk.

To appreciate the behaviourist model a little better, try this thought experiment. Imagine yourself imprisoned (you can make up your own charge) and hungry and knowing that pulling one of a number of levers in your cell wall would lead to your receiving food. On the first occasion you might try out these levers randomly until you pulled the right one but on subsequent occasions you would probably pull the correct lever straight away. You would not know, and probably would not wish to know, exactly why this worked but you would be happy so long as it led to the desired effect, the reward of food. Perhaps eventually you would salivate at the sight, or even the thought, of the food lever.

This model is quite an attractive one at first sight and, although it has been criticised as you will read below, we should not dismiss every instance of learning in this way. To give just two illustrations of what we might regard as stimulus-response learning, think of your emotional and physical responses to, firstly, waking up on the first day of your holidays and, secondly, walking into an interview room. Even the thought of a pleasant or unpleasant event can lead to a response within us, whether this is an involuntary smile or butterflies in the stomach.

In further support of the behaviourist model of language acquisition, we can easily observe that children are keen mimics who take great pleasure in hearing words repeated and repeating them themselves. However, as a model to explain the whole of language acquisition, behaviourism has received serious criticism from linguists such as Noam Chomsky (for example, Chomsky, 1959) who are collectively known as 'nativists'.

Nativist models

Nativists argue that a behaviourist model cannot give a satisfactory account of the creativity inherent in virtually all speech apart from the most trivial and banal. Look at any set of utterances that people make, say the nativists, and you will find it hard to find exact replicas of those utterances in that particular sequence. They cannot therefore be generated, the nativists object, by simple copying. Put more crudely, behaviourism might give a plausible explanation of the young child crying 'Teddy!' but not of Shakespeare's creation of *Hamlet*. Nativists believe that the capacity to learn language is innate or, as some commentators put it, hard-wired into the human being. The reason, nativists argue, that young children are so skilled at working out the language around them (and this could be any human language that they happen to be immersed in) is that this is exactly what they are programmed to do. Indeed, for some of these writers, computing terms such as 'programmed' and 'hard-wired' are not just metaphors but are chosen to make explicit just how similar human language use is to computer processes. A prominent cognitive scientist who has proposed similar ideas to Chomsky more recently is Steven Pinker (for example, Pinker, 2007). The title of one of his readable and informative books is *The language instinct* (Pinker, 1994), a term which provides us with another metaphor for the way in which many nativists see children's acquisition of language. A recurrent notion in nativist models is that there is a universal grammar and children are born with the capacity to deduce its rules as applied to their mother tongues. Look at the Reflective Task which follows for a little more about this.

REFLECTIVE TASK
REFLECTIVE TASK

Observe young children talking in the home or in an educational setting. (You will probably notice that children will talk much more readily if they feel engaged and comfortable.) Do you notice any errors (from an adult speaker's perspective) such as 'He goed there'? Do not correct children when you hear examples like this. This is a temporary phase which they will move on from. Nativist theorists often interpret this kind of error as an over-generalisation of a rule. Children realise that '-ed' is the regular suffix which changes verbs into the past tense (such as talk/talked, walk/walked, watch/watched and so on) and may wrongly apply it to all verbs, regardless of whether they are regular (like 'talk') or irregular (like 'go' which becomes 'went' rather than 'goed' in the past). What else do you notice about the way in which the children you observe structure their speech?

Nature versus nurture

Extreme behaviourist and nativist accounts might, rather crudely, be placed at opposite ends of a continuum indicating the relative effects that nature and nurture have upon language development. Behaviourist accounts would generally lie at the nurture end of this continuum, since their accounts rely so heavily upon environmental factors (although this is not to deny that children might be born with different abilities to develop their language skills), while nativist accounts are more closely aligned with nature, that is, with the resources the individual is born with. Although helpful in making some initial sense of this distinction, however, it is important to point out that very few commentators would place their models at either end of this continuum. Although it may never be possible to establish this with any certainty, most debates that involve a contrast between nature and nurture generally end with some agreement that both factors interact in complex ways and that neither accounts on its own for individual differences. One group of theorists put this nicely: *For human beings nurture is our nature* (Gopnik, *et al.*, 2001, p8; author's emphasis).

There are other explanations of language acquisition which do not fall easily into the two categories described so far and these include some very interesting current lines of research. Like the behaviourists, those who support the models in this final group (sometimes known collectively as 'empiricist' models) believe that environment has a major part to play in allowing a child's linguistic potential to be realised. However, unlike behaviourists such as Skinner, most modern theorists of this kind do not favour a straightforward stimulus–response model but see children as active agents constructing their own understanding of language.

The development of language and thought

Any exploration of the relationship between language and thought would be inadequate if it failed to take account of the theories of Jean Piaget and Lev Vygotsky, two of the giants of educational thought over the past century, who you are likely to have encountered already in your educational studies. Piaget and Vygotsky did not share the focus of the theorists that we examined in the previous section as they were less concerned with the process of language acquisition than with the development of thought. Although both men were polymaths, dealing with a wide range of topics and perspectives, it is probably useful to consider their theories as fundamentally psychological rather than linguistic. Their theories involve accounts of language use which are highly relevant to this book and some of these will be briefly examined in the next sections.

Piaget

Attitudes to the work of Piaget have swung like a pendulum over the last half century or so. His work began in the 1920s and gradually came to have enormous influence over education – particularly primary education – until, by the 1960s, his theories were thought by many to have captured, incontrovertibly, the way in which young children's thinking develops. One of the main ideas that Piaget put forward was that children actively constructed their understanding of reality. He is therefore described as a 'constructivist', along with many other educational thinkers. Constructivism is often contrasted with the idea of the child as an empty vessel, waiting to be filled by the knowledge that teachers pour in. In one form or another, constructivism is favoured by many educationalists today.

Piaget believed that young children thought about the world very differently from adults, and even from older children, and he argued that all children must go through a predetermined series of developmental stages on their journey towards mature, adult-like thinking. He called these stages the 'sensori-motor' stage, the 'pre-operational' stage, the 'concrete operational' stage, and the 'formal operational' stage. We have already discussed the difficulty of attaching precise ages to developmental milestones, since individual children vary so much, and Piaget was aware of this difficulty. However, there are some generally accepted guidelines given by Piaget and his followers which suggest that, for most children, the primary years include the middle two of these developmental stages: what he termed the pre-operational stage (which runs from about two to six or seven years) and the concrete operational stage (which runs from about seven to eleven and therefore roughly coincides with the school age-phase of Key Stage 2). A little later you will see that key elements of Piaget's scheme, including the very existence of such stages, have been hotly disputed. First, though, we must try to understand some of Piaget's ideas about the relationship between language and thought.

As we have already noted, Piaget saw all children as being engaged from birth in a project to construct a picture of reality and he saw them as 'little scientists' in this undertaking. At each stage of their development they process and try to make sense of the experiences they have, not only educational experiences but every other life experience too. Children relate these experiences to their current model of the world and generally assimilate them into this world view without undue difficulty. However, at certain critical points, assimilation is impossible for children and their experiences force them to change their world view to accommodate them. These times, when a major world view needs to change so that new information or experience can be accommodated, are key learning moments. You should note that Piaget, like many other theorists, sees cognitive conflict as an important factor in the learning process.

A famous example allows us to examine some of the differences he saw between the pre-operational stage and the concrete operational stage. Piaget claimed that one of the distinguishing features of what he termed the pre-operational stage was that children were unable to 'decentre'. They took one particular view of a situation and could consider no other. He conducted a series of experiments which tried to establish whether a child faced with a model of three mountains could imagine the viewpoint of people viewing the scene from different points (each clearly – to adult eyes – having a very different view.) Piaget's results suggested that children at the pre-operational stage of development could not do this. Their egocentricity at this age, he claimed, prevented them from seeing a situation from any viewpoint but their own.

Another famous Piagetian experiment involves presenting a child with two lines of counters, each containing the same number. When the counters in these lines are equally spaced, the child has no difficulty in seeing that each line has the same number of counters. When one line is then spread out, however, the typical response of the young child is to claim, in response to a question, that there are more counters in the longer (more spaced-out) line. Even here we might argue that the child finds the word 'more' ambiguous since it might be taken to refer to the number of counters (which has not changed) or the length of the line (which clearly has). Piaget asserted, however, that this and similar experiments demonstrated that children at the pre-operational stage had not properly understood conservation of volume, number and other mathematical concepts. Essentially, conservation here refers to the idea that things can be rearranged in any way and, so long as nothing is added or taken away, there will be the same quantity at the end as at the beginning.

Piaget's views challenged

In the 1970s, Margaret Donaldson and other researchers (see, for example, Donaldson, 1978) set up a similar experiment to Paiget's 'three mountain' experiment which was described above. The context was changed, however, to one in which a doll had to be hidden from policemen behind walls in a model. Donaldson found that the success rate of children at what Piaget would have described as the pre-operational stage was strikingly higher on this test, since it involved a more intelligible and engaging context. Critics of Piaget have also suggested that he paid too little attention to the effects of language that might be ambiguous to the child. When shown a picture of two types of flowers, say six tulips and six daisies, children were asked by Piaget, 'Are there more flowers or are there more tulips?' Young children often answered that there were more tulips although the correct answer in a strict sense was that there were more flowers. Many adults might give the wrong answer to such a question because they were confused rather than, as Piaget would claim, because they lacked the ability to simultaneously classify objects in more than one way. As Wood points out, *Questions like 'Are there more flowers or more tulips?' sound distinctly odd!* (Wood, 1998, p61).

Piaget's findings are intriguing and anyone who observes children giving answers of this kind is left with the sense that there is something about the way in which young children view the world which is different from the way that adults see it. In fact, one of the most impressive features of Piaget's views, which even his critics generally concede, is that he did not have a deficit model of young children but saw their thinking as distinctive and characterising their developmental stage rather than simply being poor adult thinking. His theories certainly highlight the complex relationship which exists between language and thought.

REFLECTIVE TASK

Look back at the Practical Task in Chapter 2 and the research which was described (see page 8). Remember the responses that the Reception class children gave to the question 'How big is your house?' which were to stretch their arms out in demonstration and to say things like 'This big'. You may have asked young children similar questions yourself as the Practical Task recommended. Followers of Piaget would claim that children of this age respond in this way because they are unable to take account of their listener's needs. They are unable, in other words, to decentre from a given viewpoint and see it from another person's point of view. Notice the responses that adults gave to the same question which seemed to take much more account of the listener's needs. (The author found that children in upper Key Stage 2 gave similar answers to adults.) Thinking back on this account and any of your observations which you were invited to make, do you feel that children in Foundation Stage and early Key Stage 1 have difficulty decentring from their own perceptions? This is a question which we will return to in Chapter 6.

Vygotsky

As Donaldson and others challenged Piaget's ideas in the 1970s and later, the pendulum of popular support gradually swung away from his theories. You will find many modern accounts which treat his work disparagingly but you should resist the temptation to conclude that Piaget has been proved wrong in every respect. Some educational thinkers have continued to support and build upon Piaget's insights and other current educationalists working in this field have continued to commend some aspects of Piaget's work even if they disagree with others (for example, Howe and Mercer, 2007). A major thinker whose work is more influential than Piaget's currently, however, is Lev Vygotsky.

Vygotsky's work is considered so relevant to the modern classroom that many trainees are misled by recent publication dates to assume that he is a contemporary writer. In fact he lived in the Soviet Union in the early part of the twentieth century and died of tuberculosis in 1934, aged only 37. The work of Vygotsky and his collaborators fell foul of the Soviet authorities and this led to a delay in its arrival in the West. When they eventually reached a Western educational audience, Vygotsky's ideas were developed by a range of important thinkers, such as Barbara Rogoff and, most notably, Jerome Bruner. Vygotsky agreed with much in Piaget's account of children's development. This is often overlooked by comparisons of the two men's work but much of one of Vygotsky's classic texts, *Thought and language* (Vygotsky, 1962), pays tribute to Piaget's analysis. Vygotsky did not subscribe, though, to Piaget's stage theory or to his views on language and the social dimension of learning. Both theorists accept the vital role of interaction with others in the learning process. For Piaget, though, since young children were egocentric and unable to decentre from their own viewpoint, any true social interaction, of the kind that adults enjoy, was not possible. Additionally, Piaget saw no real value in the talk of young children, and seems to have regarded it as an almost meaningless vocal accompaniment to activity.

By contrast, Vygotsky saw learning as an inescapably social and cultural activity and he saw language as the crucial medium through which ideas were expressed and shaped during any learning experience. Because of this emphasis on the role of language and the social dimension of learning, Vygotsky is known as a 'social constructivist'. One of Vygotsky's best-known and most influential ideas is that, if we consider children's learning potential when learning without support, and contrast that with children's potential when supported by someone more expert in that area of learning, the second potential will be considerably greater than the first. He called the gap between these two potentials the 'ZPD', generally translated as the 'zone of proximal development' (although some writers suggest that the 'zone of potential development' is a better translation). The job of teachers and other educators, therefore, is to help children to reach their greater potential through learning in a social context. Vygotsky's view of young children's language was significantly different from Piaget's too, in that he saw the language that young children used while acting as both social and self-directing. A crucial aspect of this talk, for Vygotsky, was that it was externalised thought. Through it, children regulated and commented on their actions and eventually, as they matured, this type of speech would become internalised and remain within the mind as inner speech to convert ideas into language. The more recognisable kind of speech that we use socially, on the other hand, would continue to develop and had the opposite purpose to inner speech, existing instead to convert ideas into language to be shared with others.

A key strategy that teachers can use to help children learn in the way that Vygotsky envisaged, is to 'scaffold' their learning. The seeds of this idea lie in Vygotsky's work but it was more fully developed by Bruner and others in the 1970s. The word 'scaffolding' is apt for, just as scaffolding on a building supports constructional work for as long as that support is needed, so the sort of scaffolding suggested here supports children as they learn. Practically, many activities and resources can act as scaffolding. Children embarking on a piece of writing might have a word-bank of suggested words or sentence structures; children engaged in mathematical activity might have access to useful images such as number lines or a set of number facts. When speaking to children, teachers might model some language structures which they feel it would be useful for the children to adopt. All of these devices and many more can be used to scaffold learning. Sometimes the kind of prompts and questions used by a teacher or other leader in a discussion can scaffold the talk which ensues. An important point to remember is that just as a building would not have scaffolding attached to it permanently, the scaffolding of children's learning should be available for as long as it is required but should be gently removed thereafter. Clearly, careful judgement is needed here to avoid distress caused by removing support while it is still needed, but scaffolding should be regarded as a transitional strategy and, if we want children to be confident, independent and self-reliant, we must be careful not to create a culture of dependency in our classrooms by providing more scaffolding than is needed or leaving it in place for longer than necessary.

REFLECTIVE TASK

You want the children in your Year 3 class to prepare a short radio broadcast (perhaps to be played to younger or older children in school rather than on a real radio station). The topic is an investigation they have carried out into how children spend their pocket money. You know that your class contains some children who are confident and articulate and some others who are shy and struggle to put their thoughts into words. How could you scaffold the experience for the children who will struggle so that all of the children in your class have the chance to participate to the best of their ability?

Does language shape thought?

An idea which has received a great deal of interest over the years is that our language shapes our thought and this is an idea which is extremely relevant to this book. In a crude sense this connection between language and thought is undeniable. If I tell you that a lion is charging towards you then my language will certainly shape your thinking in a way which might save your life. If we do not speak the same language then I must resort to shouting, pointing and other gestures, in the absence of words we both understand like 'Lion!' and 'Run!' (Interestingly, my facial expression will probably communicate a state of emergency very quickly, whatever our linguistic and cultural backgrounds.) The popular version of the thesis that language shapes thought, however, suggests more far-reaching connections between the two.

Relationships between language and thought

Broadly, this thesis claims that the words we use determine our thought and alter our world view. If we had different languages from one another, the thesis goes, we might think different thoughts and somehow *see* the world differently. Perhaps the most famous literary example of this is the language Newspeak which was designed by the totalitarian rulers of society in George Orwell's *Nineteen Eighty-Four* as a mechanism to enslave their citizens (Orwell, 1949). Another example you may have come across is based upon the claim that Eskimos have a large number of words for snow. Those reporting this claim often go on to argue that Eskimo thought is different because of this difference in language. This type of argument was most famously made by the American linguists Sapir and Whorf nearly a century ago (although the idea can be traced back to earlier writers) and is therefore referred to as the 'Sapir-Whorf Hypothesis'. Steven Pinker, mentioned earlier, is highly sceptical about such claims and, before setting out a detailed challenge to variations of the thesis, he suggests that:

> [t]he idea that Eskimos pay more attention to varieties of snow because they have more words for it *is so topsy-turvy (can you think of* any other reason *why Eskimos might pay attention to snow?) that it's hard to believe it would be taken seriously were it not for the feeling of cleverness it affords at having transcended common sense . . . even if an Eskimo typically does pay more attention to varieties of snow, all it would take is a shovelful of slush to get a non-Eskimo to notice the differences.*

(Pinker, 2007, pp125–26; author's emphasis)

There is another very important issue that we must consider here, and that is the extent to which the thinking of both children and adults is shaped by communication with others. In the previous section we examined the work of Vygotsky who suggested that, in an educational setting, a more expert partner could accelerate the progress of those with less expertise in a given area, through appropriate communication and scaffolding. There is a very powerful and subtle idea underlying the work of Vygotsky and others, one of which is of enormous relevance to classroom practitioners, and that is that a great deal of thought is constructed socially. An image we often conjure up is of ideas being created entirely within the confines of an individual mind. The popular idea of a genius, for example Einstein developing relativity theory while working in the Swiss Patent Office, reinforces this picture. However, while it seems self-evidently true that people do work on ideas individually, sometimes, like Einstein, to remarkable effect, a great deal of our thought is developed through communication with others. An insight into this process arises with the familiar experience of clarifying your thoughts by putting them into words and hearing others respond to them. As someone once put it 'I do not know what I think until I hear what I say.' Or, as Douglas Barnes puts it:

> *It is not that our ability to think waits upon our knowledge of language... but that the desire to communicate with others plays a dynamic part in the organizing of knowledge.*

> (Barnes, 1976, p91)

We will return to this issue in the final section of this chapter when we consider the work of Neil Mercer and the current movement towards dialogic teaching.

Language and social class

Even if the more extreme versions of the idea that language shapes thought are contentious, there are some important ways in which children's capacity to express their thoughts are affected by their language skills. It will probably be clear to you that there are great variations in the spoken language abilities of the children that you teach, no matter what age they are. While we must take great care not to underestimate the language skills of any of our children, we cannot escape the reality that they arrive at school with very different levels of linguistic skill. Many factors are likely to give rise to such differences and, once again, there is clearly an interplay of nature and nurture here. Some of this variation will probably be accounted for by the innate or natural abilities that particular children have but it seems clear too that the home experiences that children have are highly significant. While these vary in a wide range of ways, it has been recognised for many decades that social class and levels of affluence often correlate with variations in language use and with educational success.

An early investigator of these relationships was the British sociologist Basil Bernstein. The main idea that Bernstein proposed in his early work was that the language use of different social classes allowed them very different levels of access to educational success (for example, Bernstein, 1973). Put simply, Bernstein's contention was that children from middle-class backgrounds had had the opportunity to develop forms of language which enabled them to become successful in school, since these language forms were the ones most used by teachers in schools. Bernstein's theory was seen by many at the time as a crucial insight into the hidden mechanisms which led to educational disadvantage but his arguments and the ways in which they were developed by others were severely criticised by the American sociolinguist William Labov. In a highly influential article (Labov, 1969) Labov cited counter-examples to Bernstein's, from an American context, which suggested that the language of children from less affluent backgrounds was often far richer than these theories portrayed and, moreover, that much middle-class language was vacuous and lacking in intellectual substance. In Labov's view, the theories of Bernstein and associated writers amounted to a denigration of the language of less affluent children, judged from a middle-class standpoint.

So powerful were the challenges to Bernstein's ideas that they were seen by many at the time to have been completely discredited. Over time, however, this assessment has come to seem unnecessarily harsh. Bernstein himself developed and refined his theories throughout the rest of his life and, even if the linguistic structures he proposed were open to criticism, the ideas that children's language abilities could help or hinder them in school, and that this variation correlated to some extent with social background, have been returned to many times. One notable educator who contributed a great deal to our understanding of these issues was Joan Tough who, in her work for the Schools Council in the 1970s (for example, Tough, 1977), began with the idea that children enter school with language skills which render them more or less likely to succeed there. Tough and her collaborators developed a great deal of classroom practice to help teachers model language which was linguistically richer and more suited to the demands of the school.

It seems an uncontentious claim today that schools must help children to develop their language skills appropriately in order to remove barriers to educational success. Of course it is essential, in doing so, to avoid taking a negative view of underachieving groups, the so-called 'deficit' model of language which Labov and others have warned against. Changes in British society over the last half century have meant that some of our ideas of social class have had to change in the years since Bernstein first advanced his ideas. The recent *Bercow Report* (DCSF, 2008), though, makes clear that Speech, Language and Communication Needs (SLCN) exist on a very large scale and that there is a clear link between such difficulties and socio-economic background:

> *Approximately 50% of children and young people in some socio-economically disadvantaged populations have speech and language skills that are significantly lower than those of other children of the same age.*
>
> (DCSF, 2008, p13)

There are cautions that should be sounded here. The SLCN that the *Bercow Report* highlights are not identical to the kinds of difficulties and disadvantages that writers such as Bernstein and Tough were primarily concerned with, although Bercow's broad definition of SLCN makes it clear that his committee's view of this range is not confined to those children who have more extreme speech difficulties. The *Rose Report* raises similar concerns.

> *The perception of primary schools visited by the review is that more children are entering primary schools with impoverished language and poor social development. This issue was also highlighted in the Bercow report [DCSF, 2008] and in recent research...Further studies have shown how the number of books in the home influences children's 'word knowledge' and 'world knowledge'.*
>
> (DCSF, 2009, p57)

The report goes on to cite the work of cognitive scientist Maryanne Wolf, who makes important links between children's reading potential and their background experiences. This idea will be returned to in the Reflective Task on page 26 and in the final section of this chapter.

> *Unbeknownst to them or their families, children who grow up in environments with few or no literacy experiences are already playing catch up when they enter kindergarten and the primary grades... When words are not heard, concepts are not learned. When syntactic forms are never encountered, there is less knowledge about the relationship of events in a story. When story forms are never known, there is less ability to infer and to predict. When cultural traditions and the feelings of others are never experienced, there is less understanding of what other people feel.*
>
> (Wolf (2007) quoted in DCSF, 2009, p57)

It may be then that, while difficulties of this kind have often been seen as being associated with social class, this is strongly related to the poverty in which some families are forced to live. These are complex issues, though, which do not lend themselves to simple analysis. As a teacher, you should constantly try to be aware of factors which may affect your children's progress without using this information to narrow your expectations of them. You should also try to believe at all times that your children might be capable of achieving more than they are at present, since your belief in their potential is extremely important. You should strive to help them reach that potential by creating opportunities for engagement and challenge and by remaining vigilant for any sign of barriers that they might need support to overcome. These are tough challenges but tackling them will make you a better teacher, more capable of offering learning opportunities which are appropriate for your children and more sensitive to their needs.

As Maryanne Wolf suggests above, the development of reading skills can be impaired by children's experiences gained through the spoken word. One extremely important contribution you can make to children's language development in the classrooms in which you work, therefore, is to introduce and value examples of good children's literature. Reading to children is vital and many critics argue that this has diminished in importance in classrooms in recent years, partly, and somewhat ironically, because of government strategies to improve literacy which have encouraged the use of short extracts from texts for focus sessions. It is extremely important that children hear extended examples of good children's literature, sometimes including whole books spread out over many lessons. Extracts can be very useful too but a diet consisting solely of extracts deprives children of the opportunity to appreciate how good writers develop character and plot and how they sustain their use of language over the course of a book. Michael Rosen and other children's authors have been campaigning, at the time of writing, to re-establish the practice of reading whole books to children (Ward, 2009). Not all children have the opportunity to be read to outside school and for these children, as well as children new to English (whose needs will be considered further in Chapter 5), hearing good quality literature is invaluable.

REFLECTIVE TASK

Look at the two extracts below and imagine them spoken. Where would you hear language like that in each extract? What differences do you notice between them?

Extract A

Long, long ago in a land far away there lived an old woodcutter who toiled each day to make enough money to buy food for his family. One day, while walking wearily through the forest at the end of a long day, the woodcutter heard the sound of singing. Although he was hungry and tired, he lay down his axe and set off in search of the beautiful sound.

Extract B

There was this guy who cut wood for a living, dead poor he was, and he heard this woman singing while he was coming home from work.

You will probably have concluded that, although both extracts tell the same story, the first does so using language forms typical of the genre we know as fairy tales while the second is more conversational. If we want to help children to use and understand both of these styles we must ensure that they are exposed to both.

Studies of classroom talk

Although the word 'talk' is used most frequently in this book to describe classroom speech, other words and phrases are used, or have been used in the past, to refer to aspects of this, including 'oracy', 'exploratory talk', 'dialogic teaching' and 'speaking and listening'. The last of these is the term you are probably most familiar with. This varied terminology can cause trainee teachers some difficulty as they try to use key words to identify useful reference guides. We will try to clarify the meanings of some of these terms a little later but first we will put them into context as we briefly survey some major developments in this area from the 1960s up to the present day.

Early classroom research: the work of Douglas Barnes

The case for children to have better opportunities to talk in their classrooms has long been argued and there is no single point in time that this movement began. The year 1967 is a good time to begin any study of modern primary teaching since this was the year in which the extremely influential *Plowden Report* was published (DES, 1967), a report which shaped primary practice over the decades which followed. The contributions of sociologists like Bernstein and linguists such as Chomsky from around that time have already been noted but perhaps the most influential educator investigating classroom speech and the ways it could be improved was Douglas Barnes, whose insights continue to shape discussion about these issues. In a landmark book called *From Communication to Curriculum* (Barnes, 1976), he analysed the kinds of verbal interactions which take place in classrooms. He advocated a form of communication which he termed 'exploratory talk', a vital form of talk between children in which they could explore and play around with ideas as they formulated their ideas. Like many subsequent researchers, Barnes found that opportunities for children and teachers to communicate in this way, or in other ways which developed higher-order thinking, were sadly lacking in many classrooms. One of Barnes' conclusions was that:

> [a]lmost all teachers appear to use the question-and-answer routine (called the 'recitation' in the United States) as a way of controlling pupils' attention...David Scarborough showed that in lessons in London primary schools the pupils' replies became shorter as the teacher's questions became longer. When this happens it is the teacher who is structuring meaning and leaving only slot-filling to the pupils.
>
> (Barnes, 1976, pp172–3)

Barnes gives an example of such a teacher-question which Scarborough had recorded:

> What is it when the tug's doing its job that enables a big ship to move quite easily when the tug isn't pulling it?
>
> (Barnes, 1976, p173)

The expected pupil-answer to this question was 'Water'. Although we may smile at the linguistic knots into which the teacher has tied herself (and her pupils), we will see in the concluding section of this chapter that such domination of classroom talk by the teacher has been repeatedly found by classroom researchers.

Intermittent progress in oracy

In the decades following Barnes' early work, there have been a number of attempts to steer classroom teachers towards more productive forms of talk. A very important government report *A Language for Life* (more popularly known as the *Bullock Report*: DES, 1975) urged teachers to look for ways of developing children's spoken language across the whole curriculum, not simply in those lessons devoted to English. The *Bullock Report* presented teachers with a model of language development in which children would only improve their literacy skills if their spoken ability in English was developed simultaneously. This idea is a very important one for you to recognise as there has been a tendency in recent years, particularly since the introduction of the National Literacy Strategy (NLS) (DfEE, 1998), for teachers to concentrate on children's literacy skills independently of their abilities to use language orally. It should be pointed out that this tendency is not entirely due to that guidance. Both the NLS and the version of the National Curriculum at the time of writing (DfEE, 1999b) recognise the vital importance of children's spoken communication in developing literacy skills, but the increased pressure upon schools to improve children's literacy skills has led to an emphasis upon these skills (the end of key stage tests in English, for example, only assess literacy skills and do not include an assessed component in speaking and listening). As Bullock pointed out, the idea that we can develop children's literacy skills in isolation is based upon a misconception: children's (and adults') literacy skills draw upon the reservoir of language that they have built up through speaking and listening as well as through their own reading. This point has been well made more recently in the *Rose Report*.

> *'If they can't say it they can't write it'* has become something of a *cliché* which nevertheless captures the nature of the interdependencies of speaking, listening, reading and writing.
>
> (DCSF, 2009, p59)

Joan Tough's work with the Schools Council on children's speaking skills has been mentioned already. Another important Schools Council project in the 1970s led to classroom approaches which developed literacy skills through talk. Some of these approaches remain very useful and will be examined in Chapter 5. These are approaches which can usefully be described as 'directed reading–thinking activities' (Stauffer, cited in Lunzer and Gardner, 1979).

The importance of group work

Another important issue is that of group work. When you first visited a primary classroom, whether as a helper, a classroom assistant or a trainee teacher, you probably noticed the typical (though not universal) seating arrangement of tables grouped together so that groups of children – most often six – could work together. This could have led you to think that setting up effective group work is simply a matter of arranging your classroom seating plan in this way. Research has demonstrated, however, that this is not the case. The Observational Research and Classroom Learning Evaluation (ORACLE) study led by Galton and Simon in the late 1970s (and replicated later), for example, found that:

One thing that emerges quite clearly from the data is that, though pupils are typically seated in groups, for the majority of their time they work as individuals, concentrating on their own individual tasks.

(Galton and Simon, 1980, p31)

In Chapter 5 we will return to this issue and consider guidance about encouraging children to talk in pairs and in groups.

Clarifying terminology

We have already seen that there are several terms in use which refer to spoken communication in the classroom and this short section will help you to distinguish between them. The *Rose Review*, mentioned above, favours the everyday term 'speaking and listening' although it recognises that others prefer the term 'oracy'.

Some respondents preferred the term 'oracy' to 'speaking and listening skills' in the belief that this better defines the engagement in dialogue intended to advance children's thinking across the curriculum.

(DCSF, 2009, p56)

The Cambridge Primary Review (Alexander, 2009), which ran at the same time as the Rose Review and has also made recommendations about a new primary curriculum, prefers the word 'oracy'. This word has been in use since the 1960s and its similarity to the word 'literacy' is a useful reminder of the relationship between the two. Between 1987 and 1993, another major national initiative, The National Oracy Project, attempted once again to encourage classroom practitioners to create better opportunities for talk and discussion in classrooms. Following the *Rose Report*, however, 'speaking and listening' has been used in the new primary curriculum.

The word 'talk' has been used by many writers (as has 'talking' – this is indeed confusing territory) and it seems particularly suitable for the perspective taken within this book, hence its use in the book title. Unlike words like 'speaking and listening' and 'oracy', which direct our attention to the spoken language of the child, the word 'talk' directs us to the interaction between the children in the class and the adults guiding their learning, in particular the class teacher. We will turn our attention to this interaction in the final section of this chapter.

'Talking to learn' and 'dialogic teaching'

Robin Alexander has written an extremely important book in this area called *Towards Dialogic Teaching*. In it, he argues that: *Reading, writing and number may be the acknowledged curriculum 'basics', but talk is arguably the true foundation of learning* (Alexander, 2008, p9). We will return to Alexander's work below and in later chapters. We noted, in our consideration of Douglas Barnes' work earlier in this chapter, the tendency for classroom talk to be characterised by teacher direction with little opportunity for pupil contributions. This asymmetrical communication, as it is sometimes described, has been noted in many studies including Sinclair and Coulthard (1992). Research has demonstrated that exchanges between teacher and pupil frequently fall into a pattern described as 'Initiation–Response–Feedback' (IRF; some writers use E for 'Evaluation' instead of F). This is similar to what Barnes described as 'recitation' or the 'question and answer routine'. Such an exchange might proceed as follows:

Teacher: What is the capital of France? (Initiation)
Pupil: Paris. (Response)
Teacher: Good girl. (Feedback)

While exchanges of this kind are perfectly acceptable if they are part of a more varied range of interactions, you can probably see that they allow very few opportunities for pupils to demonstrate higher-order thinking if they are the dominant exchange style in the classroom.

REFLECTIVE TASK

Think about some lessons in which you have been a student. Your own school lessons are the most relevant but you may find that your memory of these is too hazy, in which case you should focus on more recent lessons you have been part of. What do you remember about the talk within these lessons? For example:

● Do you remember having much opportunity to participate and, if so, what form did your participation take?

● Were you simply given the chance to answer questions of recall or did you have the opportunity to demonstrate your thinking at a higher level? (In Chapter 5 we will consider Bloom's Taxonomy which will allow you to make more accurate assessments of this but for the moment just give your general feeling.)

● Overall, did the talk in the lesson feel more like a monologue by the teacher or a dialogue between the teacher and yourselves?

Since the late 1990s there has been a resurgence of interest in the role of talk in the primary classroom and a key objective has been to improve the nature of pupil–teacher interactions. In contrast to the teacher monologues often heard in classrooms and which you may have just recalled, one of the most influential initiatives has been to encourage 'dialogic' teaching or teaching based on more equal dialogue between teachers and pupils and among pupils themselves. Robin Alexander's very important book *Towards Dialogic Teaching* (Alexander, 2008) was mentioned at the beginning of this section and the subtitle of this book – *Rethinking classroom talk* – gives an accurate picture of its intentions.

Alexander draws upon, and draws together, a range of related projects and research in his search for more productive forms of classroom talk. One important contributor to this movement is Neil Mercer. Mercer's work, along with various collaborators, links research and curriculum development. His work is strongly influenced by Vygotsky and he builds upon the Vygotskian idea of the ZPD to develop an idea that he describes as 'intermental thinking' (Mercer, 2000). Mercer uses his own term here, the *intermental development zone* (IDZ) and its debt to Vygotsky is clear. The crucial idea, which was referred to earlier, is that thinking is more of a social activity than we might imagine and is one in which participants construct knowledge and understanding through dialogue. The teacher who is sensitive to this process can therefore enhance her pupils' thinking enormously by careful intervention and guidance.

It should be clear that the kind of classroom talk envisaged here is very different from the IRF model described above and it is this kind of talk which Alexander and others are encouraging as dialogic teaching. You may have heard the phrase 'whole-class interactive teaching' (the order of these words is different in some texts) which is an approach to teaching encouraged since the introduction of the NLS (DfEE, 1998) and the National Numeracy Strategy (NNS) (DfEE, 1999a). It would be reasonable for you to imagine that whole-class interactive teaching had put an end to the restrictive nature of classroom talk described above. Unfortunately, evidence (for example, Hardman *et al.*, 2003) suggests that this is not the case. So what does dialogic teaching propose as an alternative? A useful phrase to capture its essence is 'talking to learn' and Alexander suggests that teaching of this kind has five defining characteristics: it is *collective, reciprocal, supportive, cumulative* and *purposeful* (Alexander, 2008). In Chapter 5 we will explore the ways that you can develop these features in the talk within your classroom.

A SUMMARY OF **KEY POINTS**

> Talking is a remarkable skill. There are different theories of how children acquire language but most theorists agree that it comes about as a result of both innate factors within the child (nature) and environmental influences (nurture).

> Research has consistently shown that children's life experiences before school and outside school can help or hinder their spoken abilities. You must therefore try to enrich the language diet of all of the children in your class if they are to reach their potential.

> Along with many educationalists, Piaget and Vygotsky both believed that children construct their own picture of reality. Someone who believes this is called a 'constructivist'. Because of the importance which he attached to language and the social context in children's learning, Vygotsky is often referred to as a 'social constructivist'.

> Thinking is a social activity as well as a private activity. If you learn to structure classroom talk well and give children opportunities to demonstrate higher-order thinking then you will help them to develop this social construction of knowledge and understanding. 'Dialogic teaching' is the name which is often given to this kind of teaching which is based around dialogue between teachers and pupils rather than teacher monologues.

REFERENCES REFERENCES **REFERENCES** REFERENCES **REFERENCES** REFERENCES

Alexander, R J (2008) *Towards dialogic teaching*. (4th edition) York: Dialogos.

Alexander, R J (2009) (ed) *Children, their world, their education. Final report and recommendations of the Cambridge Primary Review*. London: Routledge.

Barnes, D (1976) *From communication to curriculum*. Harmondsworth: Penguin.

Bernstein, B (1973) *Class, codes and control. Vol 1*. London: Routledge and Kegan Paul.

Chomsky, N (1959) A review of BF Skinner's 'Verbal Behaviour' *Language*, 35: 26–58.

DCSF (2008) *The Bercow Report. A review of services for children and young people (0–19), with speech, language and communication needs*. Nottingham: DCSF.

DCSF (2009) *Independent review of the primary curriculum: final report. (The Rose Report)*. Nottingham: DCSF.

DES (1967) *Children and their primary schools*. London: HMSO.

DES (1975) *A language for life*. London: HMSO.

DfEE (1998) *The National Literacy Strategy*. London: DfEE.

DfEE (1999a) *The National Numeracy Strategy*. London: DfEE.

DfEE (1999b) *The National Curriculum: handbook for primary teachers in England*. London: HMSO.

Donaldson, M (1978) *Children's minds*. London: Croom Helm.

Galton, M and Simon, B (1980) *Progress and performance in the primary classroom*. London: Routledge & Kegan Paul.

Gopnik, A, Meltzoff, A N and Kuhl, P K (2001) *The scientist in the crib. What early learning tells us about the mind*. New York: Harper.

Hardman, F, Smith, F and Wall, K (2003) 'Interactive whole class teaching' in the National Literacy Strategy. *Cambridge Journal of Education*, 33(2): 197–215.

Harris, M (2004) First words, in Oates, J and Grayson, A (eds) *Cognitive and language development in children.* Oxford: Blackwell/Open University.

Howe, C and Mercer, N (2007) Children's social development, peer interaction and classroom learning (Primary Review Research Survey 2/1b), Cambridge: University of Cambridge Faculty of Education.

Labov, W (1969) The logic of non-standard English. *Georgetown Monographs on Language and Linguistics,* 22: 1–31. Reprinted in Keddie, N (ed) (1973) *Tinker, tailor...the myth of cultural deprivation.* Harmondsworth: Penguin.

Lunzer, E and Gardner, K (1979) *The effective use of reading.* London: Heinemann.

Mercer, N (2000) *Words and minds. How we use language to think together.* London: Routledge.

Orwell, G (1949) *Nineteen eighty-four.* Harmondsworth: Penguin.

Pinker, S (1994) *The language instinct. How the mind creates language.* New York: Harper Collins.

Pinker, S (2007) *The stuff of thought. Language as a window into human nature.* Harmondsworth: Penguin.

Sinclair, J and Coulthard, M (1992) Towards an analysis of discourse, in Coulthard, M (ed) *Advances in spoken discourse analysis.* London: Routledge.

Skinner, B F (1957) *Verbal behaviour.* New York: Appleton-Century-Crofts.

Tough, J (1977) *Talking and learning: a guide to fostering communication in nursery and infant schools.* London: Ward Lock.

Vygotsky, L S (1962) *Thought and language.* Cambridge MA: M.I.T.Press.

Ward, H (2009) Primary teachers shun whole-book reading in class. *Times Educational Supplement*, 4 September, p 18.

Wood, D (1998) *How children think and learn.* (2nd edition). Oxford: Blackwell.

Useful websites

An independent review of the primary curriculum (the *Rose Report*):
http://publications.teachernet.gov.uk/default.aspx?PageFunction=productdetails&PageMode=publications&ProductId=DCSF-00499-2009&.

4
Thinking and philosophy theory

Chapter objectives

By the end of this chapter you will have considered:

- **important insights into how children think and learn;**
- **direct and indirect influences upon children's thinking;**
- **evidence relating to 'brain-based' approaches to learning;**
- **current ideas about intelligence and 'multiple intelligences';**
- **some ideas about 'creative thinking';**
- **the importance of philosophy as a set of tools for thinking.**

This will help you to make progress towards these Professional Standards for the award of QTS:
Q1, Q5, Q7, Q8, Q10, Q18, Q25a, Q25b, Q30

Introduction

The aim of this chapter is to provide you with a brief introduction to a range of topics related to thinking and philosophy which are important for your professional development as a primary school teacher. This will include the insights of psychologists, philosophers, educationalists and others who have considered these topics. You will also gain an introduction to philosophy, although fuller exploration will follow in Chapters 6 and 7. As with Chapter 3, it is important to emphasise how compressed the discussion of the topics raised here must be. Another point of similarity with Chapter 3 is that while some of the claims made in this chapter are generally agreed, others are more controversial. In studying these two chapters you will consider some key issues from these enormous, linked areas which are extremely important for your development as a teacher.

The brain, the mind and thinking: philosophical perspectives

Where does thinking happen? This is not as straightforward a question as it might appear. Most of us today would immediately identify the brain as the part of the body most associated with thinking but many learned people in the past suspected that the brain carried out less vital functions. Modern science has, of course, produced convincing evidence that the brain is the organ which is most associated with our thinking or, to use a more technical term, with our 'cognitive' functions. We know, for example, that, if a person's brain is damaged by accident or illness, there can be immediate and devastating effects on these functions. Few people today, therefore, would seriously challenge the intimate connection between our thinking and our brains. This increase in our knowledge does not, however, fully satisfy those thinkers who have, for many centuries, sought to resolve the distinction, if there is one, between the brain and the mind. The question has been of concern to philosophers and is one of the recurrent issues in the branch of philosophy known as the 'Philosophy of Mind'. The issue is suggested in the following question: Is there anything more than the physical matter of our brains involved in our minds and our thoughts?

Many philosophers and others believe that mental activity involves the physical matter that our bodies (including our brains) are made up of and something non-material that people have at different times described as 'mind', 'soul' or 'spirit'. Mind is not, according to this view, physical matter but it somehow interacts with the physical matter of our brains in ways which give rise to our thoughts and sensations and allow us to control our bodies. Because these two interact in this way, according to this view, it is known by philosophers as a 'dualistic' theory. Many other theorists have taken a very different view about the 'mind–body' question and a term that you will see used to describe another position is 'materialism'. Materialists do not accept that the mind is a kind of pilot of the brain but suggest instead that physical matter is all that there is. When asked to explain how, for example, I can be aware, as I sit at my laptop writing these words, of what seem to me to be sensations and thoughts, materialists would deny that this is proof that I have a mind which is distinct from my brain. Somehow, they would argue, the sensations I feel and the physical events in my brain which correspond with them are one and the same.

This is as far as we will venture into this debate at this point. There are, however, several reasons why considering this issue is relevant to your development as a teacher. Firstly, children themselves are often fascinated by such profound questions and a philosophical discussion (which we will find out more about in Chapter 6) may well lead in this direction. Secondly, the issue relates to many religious views that you, your children and the adults that you work with may hold and it is useful to have thought through some of these for yourself if you are to make informed and sensitive responses if they arise in discussion. (I realise that you may have given this matter great thought already.) Finally, and more generally, considering philosophical issues yourself – doing philosophy in fact – is very good preparation for you in leading classroom discussions of the kind that this book encourages. Hopefully this glimpse of one of the most enduring problems in philosophy has whetted your appetite.

REFLECTIVE TASK

Consider the 'mind–body' issue discussed above. Which of the positions suggested (or another that you have come across) best accords with your own views at present? You may well find that your scientific and religious views come into conflict here, along with other perspectives, such as those we sometimes call 'common sense'. Does it seem to you appropriate for primary school children to consider such issues? If so, at what age might they begin to do so?

There are many books and internet sources which can introduce you to major issues in philosophy but one book that is worth considering for at least some children at upper Key Stage 2 (and perhaps for yourself) is *The Philosophy Files* by Stephen Law (Law, 2000) although the book is probably more suitable, in general, for slightly older pupils. *File 7, What is the mind?* deals in more detail with the issues raised in this section. From this point onwards in this book, the controversy will be set aside for the sake of easier reading and the mind and the brain will be referred to as though they were separate but intimately connected entities.

How does children's thinking differ from adults' thinking?

Any adult who spends time in the company of children notices that there appear to be differences between their own thinking and that of the children they are with. Moreover, the younger the children are, the more profound these differences appear to be. In Chapter 3 we examined important ideas put forward by Piaget and Vygotsky. From these (not entirely) different ideas about the development of children's minds, different teaching models have emerged. Piaget's idea of the *little scientist* and Vygotsky's ideas about the need for *guided learning* have been nicely contrasted (in Mercer and Littleton, 2007) by the metaphors of the *sandpit* (Piaget) and the *climbing frame* (Vygotsky). There are other important views of children's minds that you should consider and these include those put forward by Kieran Egan and Alison Gopnik.

Mythic and Romantic understanding: Kieran Egan's model of children's minds

Like Piaget, Egan has a stage model of children's cognitive development but, although it has a similar number of stages, Egan's model is quite different to Piaget's, stressing children's imaginative development. The two types of understanding most relevant to primary class-rooms are what he calls 'Mythic understanding' (which runs from the time the child learns to speak to about the age of seven) and 'Romantic understanding' (from about the age of seven to 14 or 15). Mythic understanding is characterised by a binary view of the world in which the child is drawn to stark contrasts such as good and evil, brave and cowardly and so on (Egan, 1993). The child is, typically, intensely interested at this stage in stories of a mythic kind which depict the world as full of heroes and villains, such as fairy stories in which a problem set out in these extreme terms (the good daughter abused by her wicked stepmother, for example) is resolved by the end of the story.

This phase of Mythic understanding eventually gives way to one that Egan describes as Romantic understanding. In this phase the notion of heroes and villains, including those with supernatural powers, is retained but this view is now overlaid by a greater sense of reality, a growing understanding of how the world works. Egan gives the example of Superman as a popular hero at this stage because his super-powers are connected, in the child's mind, to the explanatory account given in the story of how he came to have them (Egan, 1993). (In Chapter 6 we will briefly consider dramas like *Dr Who* and you should reconsider Egan's ideas at that point.) According to Egan, children are at this stage fascinated by facts about the world but often want to connect these to real-life heroes and heroines such as footballers and pop stars. These Egan sees as representing *transcendent human qualities – courage* and *nobility* being among those that he lists (Egan, 1993, p305). Egan suggests that when teachers work with children at this stage it is useful for them to link much of the learning content of their lessons to stories which allow children to make links of this kind. You will often see this in children's books. A book on the history of medicine, for example, will often focus on the lives of those who developed medicines, those who discovered cures for diseases and so on, rather than the more matter-of-fact scientific account that a text for an adult might include. Egan's views then offer us important insights into children's cognitive development and can be very useful in your classroom.

'Lanterns', 'spotlights' and counterfactual thinking in the work of Alison Gopnik

Alison Gopnik is another writer whose work opens up a window into the ways in which children's minds develop on the journey towards adulthood. One very useful book which she has co-authored was mentioned in Chapter 3 (Gopnik *et al.*, 2001) and in a fascinating, recent book (Gopnik, 2009), she draws upon recent evidence in cognitive science and a range of other sources. From these she puts together a compelling picture of how very young children, even babies, use far more imagination and reasoning than adults imagine them to be capable of. One example is the use of counterfactual thinking, the ability to imagine alternative scenarios to the ones directly presenting themselves to us, or as Gopnik colourfully describes them, the *woulda-coulda-shouldas of life* (Gopnik, 2009, p19). Through their pretence and imaginative talk and play, children explore counterfactual possibilities. Later in life, the ability to imagine such alternative realities can at times be a disadvantage since it can induce regret. (Gopnik cites research findings, for example, that silver medal winners look consistently glummer on the podium than bronze medallists because, presumably, they see themselves as having almost won the event rather than having almost missed the medals.) Overall, though, this ability is a massive advantage to individuals and to society. As Gopnik suggests:

> *Counterfactual thinking lets us make new plans, invent new tools, and create new environments. Human beings are constantly imagining what would happen if they cracked nuts or wove baskets or made political decisions in a new way, and the sum total of all of those visions is a different world.*

> (Gopnik, 2009, p23)

Gopnik's work then gives us fresh reasons to value and encourage children's play and imagination as most educationalists would urge.

Another valuable insight to emerge from Gopnik's work is her characterisation of young children's attention (which, as Gopnik points out, is very strongly related to consciousness) by comparison with adults'. Here again she cites a variety of interesting research to conclude that young children's attention can be described by the metaphor of the lantern: everything around them is of interest, their attention stretches as far as their perceptions and imagination allow. It is only with increasing age that they begin to focus their attention in ways that allow for the intense concentration shown by adults and much older children. This state Gopnik describes by another metaphor, that of the spotlight (Gopnik, 2009, p129). Clearly the switch from lantern consciousness or attention to spotlight attention is a very gradual process, beginning at one extreme when we are babies and concluding at the other extreme (if it ever does) when we are fully mature. The picture is, however, even more complex than this. Although we would not expect to see consistent focus of the spotlight kind among primary school children, instances of such focus become increasingly common as they get older and even young children are capable of intense periods of focused concentration. The switch can be the other way around too. Gopnik suggests that there are times when, even as adults, we may choose to return to a state of lantern consciousness, as we do when undertaking some forms of relaxation or meditation.

So what can we take from Gopnik's work? Certainly she offers many valuable insights into children's thinking (especially if you are working in an Early Years setting) but there are a number of practical implications which emerge from her ideas. Some are suggested in the following task.

PRACTICAL TASK PRACTICAL TASK **PRACTICAL TASK** PRACTICAL TASK **PRACTICAL TASK**

If you have number tables or spelling patterns that you want children to learn, put them in places that children will see them in the 'in-between times' of the school day. You might stick them on children's desks or tables, or display them at children's eye-level (as much of your display should be) where they will see them while queuing for lunch, for example. This may pay surprising dividends as children use their lantern attention and process them without being directed to.

Neuroscience and teaching

Science and pseudoscience

Science and medicine have given us great insights into the ways that our brains function and our understanding has developed rapidly in recent years. A similar exercise was undertaken in the Victorian era when the 'science' of phrenology was developed. The iconic illustrated phrenology head (pictured below) was developed by L N Fowler in the Victorian era and appeared to offer an external map of the functions of the brain. Unfortunately for the phrenologists, their approach did not survive the advances in understanding which followed and phrenology is now generally accepted to be a 'pseudoscience'.

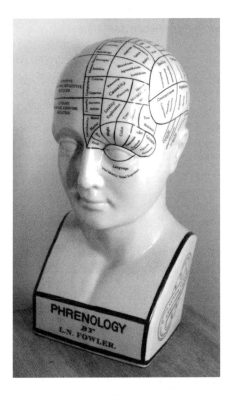

Figure 4.1 Model of head showing brain functions suggested by phrenology

In more recent times, neuroscientists have gained a great deal more understanding about the structure of the brain, and where particular functions within it are in fact located, through studies of the effects of damaged brains on the minds of their owners. This has revealed a picture which is remarkably precise in some respects, as demonstrated, for example, by the effects of brain damage on stroke and accident victims. However, the potential ability of the brain to reorganise itself in order to restore at least some lost functions reveals that it operates as a self-organising system, rather than as a set of entirely disconnected functions and that some compensation or reassignment can help to make up for deficits and damage. (This was one of the key insights to emerge from the early work of Edward de Bono (1969).) While there is a danger of overgeneralising a medical model to our classrooms, it is useful to be reminded, as teachers, of the remarkable plasticity of our brains and those of the children we teach. The static picture of the brain and mind claimed by phrenology, even if it had correctly located all of the functions it claimed to, has therefore been relegated to a historical curiosity.

The blending of neuroscience and education

Neuroscientists and cognitive scientists (a distinction which is not relevant to this enquiry) have uncovered much about the workings of the brain since the last decade of the twentieth century, aided enormously by functional Magnetic Resonance Imaging (fMRI) scans. Detailed study of this field is clearly beyond the reach of the classroom teacher but it is important that all teachers understand some of the insights emerging from this rapidly developing field as they can potentially enable them to teach more effectively. There are, however, two problems which quickly become apparent. The first is due to the newness of research in this field. Guy Claxton quotes the American neuroscientist David Fitzpatrick as saying:

> *Anything that people would say [about the brain] right now has a good chance of not being true two years from now, because the understanding is so rudimentary, and people are looking at things at such a simplistic level*

Claxton, 2008, p49).

A second problem is the prevalence of claims in educational circles of what neuroscience has allegedly proved. Paul Howard-Jones sums this up as follows.

> *... [F]or at least two decades, educational programmes claiming to be 'brain-based' have been flourishing in the UK. Unfortunately, these programmes have usually been produced without the involvement of neuroscientific expertise, are rarely evaluated in their effectiveness and are often unscientific in their approach. Perhaps this is unsurprising since, although the central role of the brain in learning may appear self-evident, formal dialogue between neuroscience and education is a relatively new phenomenon.*

(Howard-Jones, 2006, p4)

REFLECTIVE TASK

Look at the following claims and decide whether you believe them to be true. Each of them has been suggested by educationalists in recent years, in more or less extreme forms, and each is said to have been supported by neuroscience.

- Some people are left-brained and think predominantly with the left part of their brain and other people are right-brained and think predominantly with the right part of their brain. Teachers need to recognise and encourage these habits.
- Only ten per cent of our brains are ever used.
- Everyone has a particular learning style and teachers need to identify these and teach to them.
- Helping children to develop connections in their thinking is crucial to their cognitive development.
- Visualising is a powerful tool for learning.
- Talk helps children's brains to develop.
- What we eat and drink, how well we sleep and other physical and environmental factors can affect our thinking.
- Activities such as Brain Gym help children to think more effectively.
- The emotional atmosphere in the learning environment affects cognitive outcomes.

Keep your answers close to hand and consider them as you study the rest of this chapter.

The structure of the brain

The neuroscientist Paul D McLean proposed what he called the 'triune' model of the human brain some decades ago and, although it has its critics, the model has remained popular since that time. According to this view, the human brain reflects its evolution with the regions which evolved earliest (and which have most in common with less advanced species of animals) nearest the centre. The innermost region is often referred to as the 'reptilian brain' and it is responsible for some of the most primitive, but essential, cognitive functions such as the regulation of breathing and blood pressure and drives such as those for hunger and sex. Above this region is another region which is generally referred to as the 'limbic system' and which, among many other functions, has a great deal to do with our emotions. The significance of this region for thinking will be returned to later in this chapter.

The outer area of the brain is the most recently evolved region and it is this area which distinguishes the brains of humans and some other mammals from those of less advanced species. This large area is known as the 'cerebral cortex' and is the area most associated with thinking. The brain does indeed have two hemispheres, left and right, which generally (though not invariably) correspond to functions such as sensory perception and movement on the opposite side of the body to their location. (Movement of your right arm, for example, corresponds to activity in the left hemisphere of your brain.) Furthermore, it is true that there are some significant differences of function and orientation between these two hemispheres, which neuroscientists and others call 'lateralisation'. However, the claims that large parts of the brain are completely inactive or that one hemisphere operates in isolation from the other are not supported by current evidence. Blakemore and Frith, two writers who link education and neuroscience, consider:

> ... the popular idea about how many brain cells (is it 5 percent? 10 percent?) we actually use. There is no evidence for this whatsoever! Let's consider the percentage of the brain used just to tap one finger. ... [A] large proportion of the brain is activated when a finger is tapped. Tap your finger at the same time as reading this, and as well as maintaining your balance, breathing and body temperature, almost all of your brain will be active.
>
> (Blakemore and Frith, 2005, p3; authors' emphasis)

Referring to more extreme versions of the 'left-brain, right-brain' theory, Howard-Jones points out that *performance in most everyday tasks, including learning tasks, requires both hemispheres to work together in a sophisticated parallel fashion* (Howard-Jones, 2006, p16.) It seems sensible therefore to be wary of extreme characterisations of individuals as being left- or right-brained and of crude educational programmes based upon these labels. While there may be some truth in such claims, the picture is far more complex than these phrases suggest and the picture that is steadily emerging suggests that the brain is an astonishingly sophisticated organ which has evolved in ways which require both of its hemispheres to work in harmony for maximum effect, a point made forcibly by Iain McGilchrist (2009).

Another popular and widespread trend in recent years has been to identify learning styles among learners and this again, in its more extreme forms, is not one which appears borne out by neuroscientific evidence. This may seem rather surprising to you as one of the first pieces of advice which is often given to trainee teachers is the idea that they should take account of what are often called Visual, Auditory and Kinaesthetic (VAK) learning styles. The idea relates to the work of quite a number of theorists and this broader body of thought certainly contains ideas worthy of respect. The problem faced by teachers, particularly trainee teachers such as yourself, however, is that they are sometimes presented with overly simplistic versions of VAK and other models in which the cautions and qualifications that their original authors have put forward have dropped out of the picture. Psychological investigation of the VAK model raises significant doubts about its validity, certainly in an extreme form, as Howard-Jones notes. He then goes on to qualify this point in a way that we will return to in due course:

> *Of course, this does not detract from the general value for all learners when teachers present learning materials using a full range of forms and different media. Such an approach can engage the learner and support their learning processes in many different ways, but the existing research does not support labelling children in terms of a particular learning style.*

(Howard-Jones, 2006, p16)

Before we end this section, we will consider what neuroscience is revealing to us about what happens in our brains moment by moment as we think and act. To do so we must switch from the macro-level view of the brain that we have taken so far to an extreme close-up. The brain consists of cells called 'neurons' and the adult brain consists of about a hundred million of these which are constantly connecting to one another at junction points called 'synapses'. Because we have such a large number of neurons and because each neuron can have a great many synaptic connections, the number of synapses in our brains is unimaginably large. Moreover, these synapses are not fixed connections like those on a computer circuit board. Instead they are in a dynamic state, constantly being connected and reconnected as our brains process and respond to incoming information in a process known as 'synapto-genesis'.

The importance of making connections

We need to modify this picture of brain function a little further and this will lead to some very useful conclusions for us as teachers. Some neural pathways are much more firmly established than others and, whenever we learn, we strengthen the network of synaptic connections which allow us to retrieve knowledge, process new information and solve problems. A term used by some neuroscientists to describe this clustering of strengthened connections is 'template'. Andrew Curran (2008) gives a readable account of the way in which we put templates together to form larger ideas. He describes this process using the example of someone looking for their car in a car park and bringing together templates – the concept of car, the colour of my car, the memory of a scratch on my car – into a whole. Learning therefore strengthens neural connections and allows us to create new templates. You can get some sense of the significance of this discovery if you consider that your brain is in a subtle sense 'wired up differently' now to the way it was when you began to read this page. In fact the configuration of synaptic connections in your brain is changing moment by moment throughout your life. For teachers this insight is profound for it suggests that, as we help children to think and to learn and as we present them with any educational experience, we are assisting this natural process of synaptogenesis, hopefully to beneficial effect. Sadly, though, not everything children learn is beneficial or accurate – children living in a violent, dysfunctional home, for example, may 'learn' that adults are unreliable, that they are unlovable and that violence is the best way to sort out problems.

It is interesting to compare this neurological perspective on learning with a much older notion in philosophy and psychology, that of the 'schema'. Schema is a term to be treated cautiously as it has been used in different ways by many theorists, including Piaget, over the years. In Early Years education, for example, the idea of the schema is very important and practitioners will look for patterns of action, language and thought which indicate a young child's inclination towards a particular routine. A tendency observed in play for a child to move objects from place to place, to place objects inside containers or to repeatedly turn objects around might suggest that the child is inclined towards 'schemata' such as 'transporting', 'enveloping' or 'rotating'. A fuller account of this can be obtained from many sources, including the work of Chris Athey (1990). More generally among educators, however, 'schema' is used to refer to the network of connections which we establish between related ideas. A child's schema for tree, for example, might include trees that the child knows through books, by appearance, or by personal experience such as the oak, the beech and the sycamore as well as more general trees in stories, including legendary trees like the Major Oak in Sherwood Forest. Other connections might include an understanding that expressions like 'the tree of life' are connected metaphorically to the same core concept. Schemata offer the security of prior understanding but they can constrain our thinking by leading to stereotypes like 'women drivers'.

The important link between the schemata that psychologists have described and the insights into brain function which are emerging from neuroscience is that they all depend upon connections, whether we suggest that these are within children's minds or brains or both (to return to this philosophical issue momentarily). It seems reasonable to assert, therefore, that neuroscience supports the kind of teaching which stresses the importance of helping children to make connections within and across the areas of learning in which they are engaged. Support from this comes, too, from an important study carried out into effective numeracy teaching (Askew *et al.*, 1997) in which it was found that the most successful teachers were those whose approach was described as 'connectionist', helping their children to make connections across the mathematics curriculum. This conclusion seems generalisable beyond mathematics and is in line with the constructivist models of cognitive development that we examined in Chapter 3.

Another teaching and learning strategy supported by neuroscientific and other research, is visualisation. Blakemore and Frith (2005) note that visualising an object activates a large proportion of the areas of the brain that are activated when we actually see the object. They point out too that the brain appears to mirror activities observed and this can be an important aid to learning.

Helping children to mature

The role of talk is crucial to cognitive development. Robin Alexander cites evidence (Johnson, 2004; Kotulak, 1996) to show that the periods from birth to three and from three or four to ten or eleven years of age are crucially important for a child's cognitive development and that talk is vital to this process (Alexander, 2008, p13). Another crucial development as children mature is the emergence of more self-control and other aspects of what psychologists call 'executive function'. This complex and crucial set of skills is strongly associated with the development of the area of the brain known as the prefrontal cortex. Understanding the development of executive function is particularly challenging to neuroscientists but some clues about its importance have already emerged.

In the 1960s, the American psychologist Walter Mischel demonstrated that pre-school children's abilities to resist the temptation to eat a marshmallow while an experimenter left the room (the reward for this restraint being the offer of two marshmallows on the experimenter's return) was a very good predictor of future educational success. The ability of the children who resisted the single marshmallow in order to gain a higher reward later – deferred gratification – is an example of executive function being successfully utilised. Poor executive function, on the other hand, is associated with a wide range of problems, including low academic achievement and a variety of behavioural problems which can result in the individual running into serious trouble with authority in school and beyond. The key thinking skill known as metacognition, which was mentioned in Chapter 2 and will be returned to in Chapter 6, is certainly connected to executive function, so much so that some commentators have suggested that the two names refer to the same set of skills.

What sort of environmental factors affect thinking?

You will probably have concluded that the evidence from neuroscience throws doubts upon the first three claims you were asked to consider in the Reflective Task on page 38 and supports the next three. But what about the final three claims? We will consider each of these in this section. More generally, what are the conditions which we could potentially control and which either help or hinder effective thinking?

Diet, sleep and exercise

Good nutrition is likely to lead to better brain functioning, a suggestion endorsed by both of the studies referred to above (Howard-Jones, 2006; Blakemore and Frith, 2005). The same studies both confirm the importance of good quality sleep for effective thinking but Howard-Jones questions the encouragement currently given to children to drink copious quantities of water. Except when they are affected by extreme heat or while undertaking exercise, research suggests that children can judge for themselves how much water to drink and it is therefore better for teachers to encourage children to drink when they are thirsty rather than trying to insist that they drink particular quantities of water. Howard-Jones also questions the use of caffeine, which is popularly believed to improve cognitive function. Caffeine is a drink which many children consume in large quantities through certain popular drinks but research strongly suggests that excessive consumption will diminish, rather than improve, mental performance. It is also worth noting that there are food supplements and other medications appearing on the market which are designed to enhance cognitive function and these are likely to increase in the future (Howard-Jones, 2006, pp10 and 19; Blakemore and Frith, 2005, pp185–86.) The debate about their use is likely to be a philosophical as well as a medical one.

One very popular classroom practice which supporters claim improves cognitive function is the movement-based practice known as 'Brain Gym'. Howard-Jones suggests that the claims made about how Brain Gym works seem *unrecognisable within the domain of neuroscience* and suggests that the improvements which seem to be associated with the practice *may work because exercise can improve alertness* (Howard-Jones, 2006, p16). Brain Gym may be useful therefore but perhaps no more useful than a vigorous PE session.

Neuroscience and special educational needs

Future research is also likely to shed useful light on a range of conditions which impede children's educational progress, such as Attention Deficit Hyperactivity Disorder (ADHD), dyslexia, dyspraxia and dyscalculia, each of which may (or may not) turn out to have identifiable, neurological components. An important note of caution should be sounded here about the risk of taking too deterministic a view of labels given to children with such cognitive difficulties. There is always an interaction between those factors that are innate and those factors that are environmentally based and which therefore have the potential for change. Scientists are currently investigating these links in an area called 'epigenetics'. If teachers lose hope in remediation, believing that a child is genetically destined to have such difficulties, then that partial and faulty neuroscientific insight may well become a self-fulfilling prophecy. This risk is summed up by Howard-Jones in an article summarising a survey of trainee teachers' attitudes to neuroscientific issues.

> [K]nowing that a pupil has ADHD, dyscalculia or dyslexia, without scientific understanding of what that means, can diminish a teacher's belief in their potential to bring about positive change, as if the label indicates some biological barrier. In contrast, modern scientific perspectives avoid biological determination, emphasise the important role of environmental influences such as education, and highlight the enduring possibility of mitigation too.
>
> (Howard-Jones, 2009, p20)

We will leave neuroscientific research aside for the moment and consider a motivational theory that pre-dates this research and which has important, indirect implications for your encouragement of children's thinking. There is, though, an important link between this theory and the kind of evidence we have been considering which will be pointed out in this section.

The role of the emotions on motivation

In the middle of the twentieth century, psychologist Abraham Maslow published a theory of motivation and learning which has been extremely influential in classrooms ever since. Maslow suggested that human needs can be viewed as a hierarchy. From highest to lowest, Maslow's hierarchy is as follows:

- self-actualisation needs;
- esteem needs;
- belongingness and loving needs;
- safety needs;
- physiological needs.

(From Maslow, 1954)

According to Maslow, no individual can properly engage with a need if other needs lower in the hierarchy have still to be satisfied. The most basic physiological needs of food, air and so on must be met first or they will divert the individual from any other pursuit. The same is true if any other need, for love or esteem for example, is not met. The highest set of needs are described as 'self-actualisation needs' which are the highest pursuits that individuals can engage in, pursuits in which their abilities are fully harnessed and from which they can obtain the highest levels of satisfaction and fulfilment. Although these could include virtually any pursuit – dancing, painting, mountain-climbing, for example – they could also include the kind of high-level engagement which can happen when children and adults are involved in challenging forms of thinking. The usefulness of this theory is that it reminds us, as teachers, that such engagement can easily be jeopardised if a child is distracted by, for example, fear, hunger or emotional insecurity.

Maslow's theory has been criticised and some deny his claim that needs are related to one another in this hierarchical fashion. Even if it is only valid at a more basic level, however, it should remind you that children's circumstances and states of mind are likely to interfere with their ability to think and concentrate on work you may put before them. Let us consider an example. You may well have observed or worked in a school which has a breakfast club, serving breakfast to children who need it before school begins. In removing the pain of hunger, the breakfast club is helping children to concentrate better since, according to Maslow's theory, the satisfaction of that basic physiological need allows children to deal with higher-order needs.

More recently, neuroscientific research appears to offer support for Maslow's ideas. You will recall from the discussion on page 39 that the limbic system has a very significant role in the management of our emotions. It would be quite natural, therefore, to assume that it has no part to play in cognitive events. A number of theorists, however, such as Weare (2004) and Curran (2008), draw upon neuroscientific research which indicates the importance of the limbic system in cognition. Far from our emotions and cognitions being divorced from one another, as many had previously believed, it seems that how we feel has a profound effect upon how we think. The psychological model that Maslow first put forward well over half a century ago, therefore, and which has seemed intuitively sound to many educators ever since, now appears to correlate with the insights we are gaining from neuroscience. Furthermore, it is starting to seem that those who lack (for medical reasons) normal access to their emotions can find themselves incapable of decision-making. Lehrer makes this argument (2009) citing the tragic example (from Damasio, 1995) of a patient who had lost all emotion following surgery and was virtually incapable thereafter of making the simplest decision. As with the earlier consideration of left versus right brain characterisations, we are driven to a similar conclusion: both logic and emotions are necessary for healthy thinking. This discovery is a serious challenge to a long-standing assumption within society that we need to subdue our emotions if we are to think clearly and decisively, an assumption that has often worked to the disadvantage of women and girls who were characterised as being too emotional for responsible positions which required such clear thinking. There is a link too with the idea of emotional intelligence which we will return to towards the end of this chapter.

REFLECTIVE TASK

Draw a line to represent, at one end, environmental factors affecting learning that teachers have some control over and, at the other end, factors that they cannot control. Consider the environmental factors discussed above and try to place them on this line. You will probably have put children's sleep patterns at the end of the line which represents those factors that are beyond your control and a range of factors affecting children's comfort, physical safety and security at the end which represents those factors more under your control. What about issues like a child's sense of belonging which Maslow identifies as a crucial need? How much direct control can you have over this yourself? Should it be closer to the middle of the line to represent a factor that you might have partial control over, at least in terms of a child's sense of belonging to a class or school community? Remember that even in situations that you cannot directly control, such as a child's out-of-school diet, there are ways in which you may have an important influence. Think carefully about the kind of influence that you would like to have. We will return to broader issues like this in Chapter 8.

Now read the following Classroom Stories and consider whether Maslow's theory might help the teachers involved to understand their children's behaviour and help the children to engage more successfully with their school work.

CLASSROOM STORY 1

Amy's Year 1 class contains a child whose family is grieving, following the sudden death of a family member, and Amy is concerned that the child in her class does not appear to be getting enough emotional support from the family at present. She has noticed that the child will not concentrate on school work but instead seems to spend the day interacting with her friends and becoming extremely unhappy whenever she has a disagreement with them.

CLASSROOM STORY 2

Kevin has a number of children from asylum-seeking families in his Year 3 class and he has asked to speak to the father of one boy about a general concern that the boy has not settled into the work he has been asked to do and a more specific concern about an incident that day. Kevin noticed that when a bench fell over with a loud bang during a PE lesson the boy spun round and looked terrified. The father explains that this is probably because the family were frequently exposed to the sound of gunfire before they left the country in which they used to live.

Which of Maslow's 'needs' are not being met for these children?

Some perspectives on intelligence

What is intelligence? You have probably realised by now that questions which sound straightforward and obvious in education rarely turn out to be so simple and this question is certainly no exception. It is, however, another crucial question for you, as a trainee teacher, to consider and is crucial to this study of thinking. A fundamental issue is whether intelligence describes a single attribute which underlies a range of abilities or whether it describes a set of interconnected abilities. One dictionary definition of intelligence is: *the capacity for understanding; ability to perceive and comprehend meaning* (Butterfield *et al.*, 2003, p844).

Many other definitions have been offered, however, and the list of potential definitions seems endless.

Tests of children's (and adults') intelligence have been around for quite some time. At the beginning of the twentieth century, the Binet-Simon test was devised. Intended to distinguish between those children who should be in ordinary classrooms and those who would be better placed in special schools because of their intellectual difficulties, this test was the forerunner of modern Intelligence Quotient (IQ) tests such as Stanford-Binet and Wechsler. Words like 'idiot', 'moron' and 'imbecile', which would today be seen as terms of abuse if applied to a child, emerged from these early tests and at that time had quite precise meanings. An 'idiot', for example, was a person with an IQ score below 30, the average or norm in such tests being a score of 100. Thankfully terms like these, along with others such as 'mentally retarded', 'backward' and 'mentally subnormal', have dropped out of modern, professional language but there are still important issues remaining for teachers concerning the implications of testing and the words we should attach to children as the Reflective Task below suggests.

REFLECTIVE TASK

In 2007 the online version of a national newspaper ran the following headline about the relationship between wealth and educational attainment:

Brightest poor children do worse than wealthy but dim classmates

Under what circumstances (if any) do you think it would be acceptable for a teacher to use the word 'bright' to describe children? What about the word 'dim'? Is there a difference between the words you might use in front of children and those you would use with colleagues or parents and, if so, is this justifiable? When you use terms to describe children's competence do you remind yourself that you are not defining these children completely but simply describing particular attributes that you believe they have? While many obviously offensive terms, such as those mentioned above, have dropped out of professional use, you should be careful in your use of terms like 'special needs children'. A slightly modified term like 'children with special educational needs' reminds us that this is not a complete description of any child but is a reference to a particular set of needs, and entitlements, that children in our care may have and that we, as their teachers, need to be aware of at times. Language, as we saw in Chapter 3, can have a serious effect on our thinking.

Early IQ tests were based on the notion that there existed a 'general intelligence', referred to as 'g', which underlay a range of competences. IQ tests have for many years been criticised for their cultural bias and for taking too narrow a view of what we call intelligence. To claim that they give no guide to intelligence, though, however we define it, is clearly an over-statement. However cautiously we must regard it, an IQ score clearly tells us something about an individual.

Such tests are sometimes used by prospective employers to identify the suitability of applicants for particular jobs and, as you know, schools use a wide variety of tests in assessing children's aptitudes and achievements. Some tests rely quite heavily on recall of information and this can have effects on the teaching of children prior to such testing. It is also worth noting the widespread enjoyment of activities involving (largely) recall across society, from pub quizzes to TV shows like *Mastermind*, *Who Wants To Be A Millionaire?* and *University Challenge*. Many tests used in schools, however, test other aptitudes such as the use and application of knowledge and these require various thinking skills to be demonstrated. This should remind you of the issue raised in Chapter 2 about the impossibility of direct observa-tion, and hence assessment, of thinking skills. These can only ever be inferred from a child's performance on a particular task. Some tests – for example the Cognitive Abilities Tests (CATS), which are commonly used to assess children on their arrival in secondary schooling – are much closer to traditional IQ tests in assessing thinking skills in three domains: words, numbers, and shape and space. These CATS are popular among secondary practitioners since the three areas of thinking skills assessed are among those which are most needed for educational success. Testing in this way, it is argued, allows for an early assessment of children's strengths and of the areas in which they will need particular support if they are to achieve their potential. There are of course counter-arguments about the scale and implications of testing in schools in this country.

Some critics have also pointed out the narrowness of what we measure (and hence value) through such tests. One influential critic of this kind is Howard Gardner, who introduced a radical challenge to traditional views of intelligence when he published *Frames of mind*, the book in which he first proposed his model of *multiple intelligences*, in 1983. Gardner's model has had enormous impact in classrooms around the world and we will examine it in the next section, in which we will also reconsider learning style theory.

Multiple intelligences and learning styles

Frames of mind is a long and elegant book and there are dangers, as there are with all theories, in summarising it too crudely. In essence, however, Gardner considers various conceptions of intelligence which have existed over time and finds the conventional academic definitions too restrictive. Gardner suggests the following, broader view.

> To my mind, a human intellectual competence must entail a set of skills of problem solving – enabling the individual to resolve genuine problems or difficulties *that he or she encounters and, where appropriate, to create an effective product – and must also entail the potential for* finding or creating problems – *thereby laying the groundwork for the acquisition of new knowledge.*
>
> (Gardner, 1983, p60; author's emphasis)

This redefinition of 'intelligence' allowed Gardner to propose seven intelligences which he described as:

- bodily-kinaesthetic;
- interpersonal;
- verbal-linguistic;
- logical-mathematical;
- intrapersonal;
- visual-spatial;
- musical.

Later, naturalistic intelligence was added to this list.

While some of Gardner's intelligences – verbal-linguistic and logical-mathematical in particular – are reasonably similar to the cognitive areas assessed through traditional IQ tests, others seem of a radically different nature. Critics have seized upon Gardner's use of the term 'intelligence', asking how, for example, bodily-kinaesthetic or musical aptitudes can be counted as forms of intelligence. Objections to Gardner's model have been raised on both psychological and philosophical grounds (see, for example, White, 2002) and the apparent lack of a solid, neuroscientific basis for his claims has also been questioned. Nonetheless, Gardner's ideas have been extremely popular within schools and even critics such as White give Gardner some praise:

> Gardner was right to challenge the identification of intelligence with what IQ tests test, and to claim that it takes more varied forms than the linguistic and logico-mathematical abilities required by those tests. But he goes adrift in trying to

pigeonhole this huge variety within his seven or eight boxes. His success in opening teachers' and project workers' eyes to new possibilities deserves our gratitude.

(White, 2002, p95)

Gardner himself has expressed misgivings about some of the ways that his ideas have been interpreted in educational settings and, in a more recent interview, he distilled the two fundamental points that he felt should be taken from his work. *One that kids are different from one another and that you should personalise as much as you can. Two, when you teach something, you should teach it in lots of different ways* (Passmore, 2006, p21). In the same interview, Gardner offered some thoughts about learning styles, confessing that he was *dubious that [they] exist* (Passmore, 2006, p20). At this point it is appropriate to recall the comment by Paul Howard-Jones, cited on page 40 (Howard-Jones, 2006, p16), about the value for all learners of presenting our teaching in a varied and, as we can usefully describe it, a multi-sensory way. Howard-Jones is making similar points about learning styles to those made by Gardner about multiple intelligences and this amounts to good advice for you as a trainee teacher. It has probably become apparent to you that trying to identify the particular learning styles and intelligences of children you teach is a problematic matter. There is also another dilemma: even if we could be completely confident that Child A had a particular learning style and combination of intelligences should we concentrate our input on those or on the learning styles and intelligences which were less prominent and perhaps less well developed? (What do you think a football coach working with a player who had a very strong right foot and a very weak left foot would want the player to work on – the stronger foot, the weaker foot or both feet?)

These reservations certainly do not mean that you should ignore the insights which these theories offer. In my own view, the most important lesson to be taken from learning styles theory is that we should always endeavour to vary the ways that we teach children and the learning opportunities that we offer them. This is neatly summed up in the *Final Report of the Cambridge Primary Review* as V, A and K rather than V, A or K (Alexander, 2009, p97). We can of course observe our children and try to identify their learning preferences as part of the full range of capabilities that they have but this is not the same as labelling their learning styles. The most important lesson to be taken from Gardner's multiple intelligences theory is that it forces us to question what is valued most highly by schools and by society. Unless those who have what he describes as musical or bodily-kinaesthetic intelligences are at the top of their professions, for example, they are unlikely to be rewarded – or regarded – as highly as those with high verbal-linguistic or logical-mathematical intelligences. There is a serious ethical and political debate to be had about these issues. If multiple intelligence theory leads to greater recognition of the contributions that different talents make to society and if it leads to more opportunities to develop that range of talents, it will be enormously valuable to countless children in our schools whose talents are often overlooked or under-valued.

Other ways of thinking and feeling

A linguistic problem is that the only word we have to distinguish what is not rational from what is rational is the word 'irrational' and this word has many unfavourable connotations. If you jot down a few associations quickly, they are likely to relate to poor choices and decision-making, over-emotional responses, superstition and so on. However, on page 44 we saw that our emotions appear to play a very significant role in good thinking. Daniel

Goleman made famous an idea which is related to Gardner's multiple intelligence theory and that is the notion of 'emotional intelligence' which has already been mentioned. Building upon Gardner's theories, Goleman (1996) argues that the qualities which will be needed increasingly by individuals in future societies are not the academic abilities traditionally valued by our education systems but the range of interpersonal skills and awareness which allow people to co-exist peacefully and to negotiate their objectives. Goleman terms this set of abilities emotional intelligence and this has led to the notion of an Emotional Intelligence Quotient (EQ). In fact, Goleman's best-selling book *Emotional Intelligence* carries the provocative subtitle: *Why it can matter more than IQ*. A term similar to emotional intelligence which you will commonly hear in schools and other educational settings is 'emotional literacy'. There are large areas of the primary curriculum, areas we might refer to collectively as the 'affective curriculum', which are concerned with developing children's emotional skills, such as empathy, compassion and communication.

In the new primary curriculum these areas will be addressed within the Essentials for Learning and Life area called Personal and Emotional Skills and Social Skills and, to some extent, within the Area of Learning called Understanding physical development, health and wellbeing.

There are links too with the subjects labelled Citizenship and Global Citizenship, the Social and Emotional Aspects of Learning (SEALS) initiatives and to Gardner's *interpersonal* and *intrapersonal intelligences*. There are a variety of classroom practices through which these skills can be fostered. Circle time is one, but another approach which will be dealt with in detail in Chapter 6 is P4C which, as you will see, is both a thinking skills programme and a programme to develop social and interpersonal skills.

Before concluding this section and this chapter, there is one more important issue to consider. Although rational, logical skills are clearly very important and will be a major focus in your lessons, there are other ways of thinking which are not as rational but which are extremely important and, often, highly productive. The thinking shown by artists is one example. Often this results in ideas which challenge or defy conventional thinking and often, too, artists themselves have little idea where these ideas have come from. We use words like creativity, inspiration and intuition to describe the processes which lead to such outcomes. Some thinkers, such as Edward de Bono (1985) believe that Western thought has been dominated by a style that is based too strongly on logical, adversarial thought since the time of the Ancient Greeks and he, like others in this field, seek to open up children's thinking in more creative ways. Guy Claxton, whose work has already been mentioned, has written about the important part that our subconscious mind – Claxton (1997) uses the term 'under-mind' – plays in helping us as we wrestle with problems. There are many examples of intellectual breakthroughs occurring while their originators were not consciously thinking about them and we all know that sleeping on a problem can often lead to a productive way forward. Try to bear these ideas in mind when you are teaching and organising your lessons. Often this will mean allowing more time for a problem to be worked on than you might have originally planned or finding ways of helping children move forward and move past 'blocks'. This depends on the development of qualities of mind as much as particular problem-solving strategies and we will examine these in the next chapter. Finally, without seeking to attach labels of any kind, encourage your children (and yourself) to notice particular thinking habits that they have and the strengths and weaknesses of these habits that they have noticed.

A SUMMARY OF **KEY POINTS**

> Thinking is intimately connected to brain activity although there is no agreement about whether the mind is any more than the sum of activity in the brain. Neuroscientists are constantly discovering insights into how our brains work and some of these insights are extremely important for teachers to be aware of.

> Not every approach that claims to be 'brain-friendly' is supported by current evidence. It is prudent for teachers to have an interested but critical attitude to emerging practice of this kind.

> Intelligence is an important but problematic concept. Howard Gardner's ideas about multiple intelligences lead us to a broader view of human capabilities.

> Our emotions appear to play an extremely important part in our ability to think well.

REFERENCES REFERENCES **REFERENCES** REFERENCES **REFERENCES** REFERENCES

Alexander, R J (2008) *Towards dialogic teaching*. (4th edition). York: Dialogos.

Askew, M, Brown, M, Rhodes, V, Johnson, D and Wiliam, D (1997) *Effective teachers of numeracy.* London: King's College.

Athey, C (1990) *Extending thought in young children. A parent-teacher partnership.* London: Paul Chapman Publishing.

Blakemore, S J and Frith, U (2005) *The learning brain. Lessons for education*. Oxford: Blackwell.

Butterfield, J et al (2003) *Collins English Dictionary*. (6th edition). Glasgow: HarperCollins.

Claxton, G (1997) *Hare brain tortoise mind. Why intelligence increases when you think less.* London: Fourth Estate.

Claxton, G (2008) *What's the point of school? Rediscovering the heart of education.* Oxford: OneWorld Publications.

Curran, A (2008) *The little book of big stuff about the brain*. Carmarthen: Crown House Publishing.

Damasio, A (1995) *Descartes' error.* New York: Penguin.

de Bono, E (1969) *The mechanism of mind*. London: Penguin.

de Bono, E (1985) *Six thinking hats.* London: Penguin.

Egan, K (1993) The other half of the child, in Lipman, M *Thinking children and education*. Dubuque, Iowa: Kendall-Hunt Publishing Company.

Gardner, H (1983) *Frames of mind. The theory of multiple intelligences.* London: Fontana.

Goleman, D (1996) *Emotional intelligence. Why it can matter more than IQ*. London: Bloomsbury.

Gopnik, A (2009) *The philosophical baby. What children's minds tell us about truth, love & the meaning of life.* London: Bodley Head.

Gopnik, A, Meltzoff, A N and Kuhl, P K (2001) *The scientist in the crib. What early learning tells us about the mind.* New York: Harper.

Howard-Jones, P (2006) *Neuroscience and education. Issues and opportunities*. Teaching and Learning Research Programme. Downloadable from: www.tlrp.org/pub/documents/Neuroscience%20Commentary%20FINAL.pdf

Howard-Jones, P (2009) Mind where you go. *TES Magazine*, 30 January, pp. 19–20.

Johnson, M (2004) *Developmental cognitive neuroscience.* (2nd edition). Oxford: Blackwell.

Kotulak, R (1996) *Inside the brain: revolutionary discoveries of how the mind works*. Kansas City: Andrews McMeel Publishing.

Law, S (2002) *The philosophy files*. London: Orion Children's Books.

Lehrer, J (2009) *The decisive moment. How the brain makes up its mind*. Edinburgh: Canongate Books.

Maslow, A H (1954) *Motivation and personality.* New York: Harper and Row.

McGilchrist, I (2009) *The master and his emissary: the divided brain and the making of the Western world.* London: Yale University Press.

Mercer, N and Littleton, K (2007) *Dialogue and the development of children's thinking. A sociocultural approach.* Abingdon: Routledge.

Passmore, B (2006) MI: Mission Impossible? *TES Magazine*, 24 November, pp. 20–21.

Weare, K (2004) *Developing the emotionally literate school*. London: Paul Chapman.

White, J (2002) *The child's mind*. London: Routledge Falmer.

Useful websites

Centre for Neuroscience in Education, University of Cambridge:
www.educ.cam.ac.uk/centres/neuroscience.

Oxford Cognitive Neuroscience-Education Forum:
www.brookes.ac.uk/schools/education/rescon/ocnef/ocnef.html.

5
Classroom strategies to develop talk

Chapter objectives

By the end of this chapter you will have considered:

- **how to encourage productive talk in your classroom through the principles of dialogic teaching in group, paired and whole-class talk;**
- **the value of Kagan structures and other approaches to co-operative and collaborative learning;**
- **ways to improve questions and answers in your classroom;**
- **the use of Bloom's Taxonomy to encourage high-level thinking;**
- **the use of Drama and role play to stimulate productive talk;**
- **strategies for working with bilingual children.**

This will help you to make progress towards these Professional Standards for the award of QTS:

Q1, Q4, Q5, Q7a, Q8, Q10, Q18, Q19, Q25a, Q25c, Q30

Introduction: improving the balance of talk in the classroom

What does dialogic teaching look like in the classroom?

You will remember that Chapter 3 ended with an introduction to the powerful notion of dialogic teaching, an approach to classroom talk currently strongly advocated by many educationalists, notably Robin Alexander (2008). Dialogic teaching is a pedagogy which aims to help teachers provide more opportunities for high-quality talk in their classrooms by improving the balance of strategies that teachers use. It offers you the opportunity to create sound foundations in your classroom practice upon which a range of other good practices can be overlaid. Alexander suggests that, as we look at the approaches to talk which teachers adopt, we should look out for five key features which collectively mark out a particular style as dialogic teaching. He says that:

> *[i]n a nutshell...dialogic teaching is:*
> - collective*: teachers and children address learning tasks together, whether as a group or as a class, rather than in isolation;*
> - reciprocal*: teachers and children listen to each other, share ideas and consider alternative viewpoints;*
> - supportive*: children articulate their ideas freely, without fear of embarrassment over 'wrong' answers; and they help each other to reach common understandings;*
> - cumulative*: teachers and children build on their own and each other's ideas and chain them into coherent lines of thinking and enquiry;*
> - purposeful*: teachers plan and facilitate dialogic teaching with particular educational goals in view.*

> (Alexander, 2008, p28)

You should notice that Alexander's criteria relate as much to teacher attitude and classroom ethos as they do to teaching styles. He is not suggesting that there is only one model of talk which would satisfy these criteria and observes that skilful teachers develop a repertoire of strategies which they can select from in the different circumstances they find themselves. Based on extensive international studies in classrooms, Alexander identifies the following five strategies (Alexander, 2008).

Five classroom strategies

In Chapter 3 we described the commonly observed exchange of questions and answers, such as the routine sometimes described as the IRF (see page 29). This strategy is the first identified by Alexander and is known as *recitation*. A second familiar routine is an approach described by Alexander and others as *rote*. This is the kind of teaching that might occur during a maths lesson, for example, when the teacher wishes the children to practise a number table. The third strategy which is commonly found in classrooms is *instruction* or *exposition*. There are many situations in which this approach might be in evidence, such as during lessons in art, PE or science, when the teacher is guiding children towards a new skill.

Even though the first three strategies described provide fewer rich opportunities for the development of children's talk than other approaches might, all three have their place in the good teacher's repertoire. What is vitally important if you wish to improve your teaching, however, is to make sure that the fourth and fifth of the strategies Alexander has observed – *dialogue* and *discussion* – are integral parts of your teaching. These, Alexander suggests, are the strategies most likely to be missing in the British primary classroom. There is some overlap between these last two approaches in that both describe situations in which children's contributions are built upon to develop constructive thinking. We will deal here with dialogue in relation to whole-class teaching and with discussion in relation to groups later in this chapter.

PRACTICAL TASK PRACTICAL TASK **PRACTICAL TASK** PRACTICAL TASK **PRACTICAL TASK**

The purpose of this exercise is for you to audit your current approach in order to evaluate the opportunities which children currently have to engage in talk during the whole-class periods in your teaching. This is, of course, hard to do and your memory is likely to give an incomplete picture. You should therefore ask a colleague with whom you have a good working relationship to observe you teaching a lesson and feed back to you honestly, using the following questions as a guide.

- Roughly what was the balance of questions asked by you and by the children?
- Were the children's questions (if there were any) about significant content issues or were they mostly procedural (about the correct layout of their work, for example)?
- Did all of your questions require simple recall of facts or did some of them require more considered answers?
- Did you allow much thinking time before children answered?
- Were there long periods when you were speaking without interruption, periods which sounded like monologues?

What did this analysis reveal? You may have been pleased by the results or you may have discovered that you dominated the classroom exchanges and offered only restricted opportunities for children to contribute. Over the next few pages we will consider a few strategies which should help you to adjust this balance.

Better questions

You have probably recognised already that questions are vitally important for teachers. Many professionals use questions but they do not all use them in the same way. Consider the different ways that these three professionals would use questions in their work:

- a barrister in a court of law;
- a doctor in the surgery;
- a teacher in the classroom.

Let us first consider the barrister and the doctor. While the doctor uses questions to assist in diagnosis ('How long have you had these pains?'), a barrister uses questions to establish the truth – or, perhaps more accurately, the barrister's preferred version of the truth – for the benefit of the jury ('How was the defendant behaving when you entered the room?'). For obvious reasons, the barrister can encounter considerable reluctance to answer questions, whereas truthfulness is assumed in the doctor's surgery. (There are exceptions to this, of course, such as the responses which might be given to the doctor's question 'How much do you drink?') The doctor's questions are genuine searches for information, whereas, in general, the barrister is already aware of the answer which a witness is likely to give but wishes this answer to be publicly stated.

Generally, the teacher, like the doctor, does not know the answer that will be given to a question although, like the doctor, professional expertise allows the teacher to anticipate a range of potential answers that children may give and the clues these answers will give about their understanding. The teacher will also ask questions in order to encourage children to participate actively in the lesson. Clearly, the type of question asked affects the answers which can be given. An important distinction which you have probably come across before is between open questions and closed questions. Open questions allow for a range of answers, like this one:

Question A: How do you think the main character felt when his mother was taken prisoner?

Closed questions, on the other hand, invite a much narrower range of answers, often only one, as in this question:

Question B: What is five times three?

The distinction between open and closed questions is more complex than it seems at first sight, however. There are questions which, although linguistically closed, do in fact invite higher-level thinking and are therefore equivalent to open questions, for example 'Should people eat meat?'. A good indicator of such a question is that it often leads to an initial response like 'That would depend...'. It should be apparent, though, that open questions like Question A generally demand a higher level of thinking than closed questions like Question B and you might therefore imagine that you should only ask questions of this kind. The evidence from research, however, challenges this common-sense assumption. Askew and Wiliam analysed a range of classroom research (Askew and Wiliam, 1995) from a maths teaching perspective (though these findings seem generalisable across the curriculum) and they identified a number of points which you should bear in mind when you are considering your use of questions.

- A blend of higher-level and lower-level questions is generally better than just asking questions of the same type. Lower-level questions can test children's recall while higher-level questions can test their understanding.
- Adjusting the length of time you pause before taking an answer, something referred to as 'wait time' or 'thinking time' (the second term is used in this book), can have very significant effects on the quality of responses to a question and can allow more children to participate. Research suggests that most teachers pause for less than one second before taking an answer. Extending thinking time to just three seconds, after asking a question which requires high-order thinking, can make a significant difference but you should avoid leaving such a pause after every question as this can actually *decrease* engagement.
- Posing a question as a statement can be a very useful strategy. In a maths lesson for example, rather than asking a question like 'Can you have two rectangles with different areas but with the same perimeter?' you might say, 'A child in another class said that you couldn't have two rectangles that had the same perimeter but different areas. Talk to your partner and decide whether you agree with her.'

(Summarised from Askew and Wiliam, 1995)

At an even more fundamental level, if you would like your teaching to move closer to Alexander's picture of dialogic teaching, you should consider the hidden assumptions in your class about who can pose questions, answers and other contributions. Mercer and Dawes suggest that the implicit ground rules which often exist in classrooms include the following.

- *Only a teacher can nominate who should speak.*
- *Only a teacher may ask a question without seeking permission.*
- *Only a teacher can evaluate a comment made by a participant.*
- *Children should try to provide answers to teachers' questions which are as relevant and brief as possible.*
- *Children should not speak freely when a teacher asks a question but should raise their hands and wait to be nominated.*

Children who call out an answer without being asked are breaking a rule, and their contribution may thus be treated as 'invisible' until they have been formally asked to speak.

(Mercer and Dawes, 2008, p58)

Of course Mercer and Dawes are not suggesting that teachers set out to create this set of rules. As you have probably realised, however, the processes by which classroom ethos and teacher expectations are created are subtle and you should always be alert to the conditions which may have evolved in your classroom without your being aware of them. Working to change such norms within classrooms is a central part of what Alexander and others are arguing for when they advocate dialogic teaching.

Improving answers

We will turn our attention now from questions to answers. Although you can never control children's answers to your questions, you can do a lot to ensure that these are of as high a quality as possible. As well as considering the hidden norms and expectations in your classroom, as you were advised to do in the previous section, you should think about the ways in which children are given opportunities to answer. We have already noted the impact that adjusting thinking time can have but the way in which you accept answers may be more patterned than you think. The default strategy for most teachers is to encourage children to raise their hands when bidding to answer. This strategy has its place but it has limitations too. Without realising it, you may be inviting more responses from girls than boys (or vice versa) or from those children you perceive to be more able or more confident. The 'hands-up' strategy also prevents you from gaining a picture of the answers that are not selected. There are many alternatives which you should consider, including the following, and a mixture of strategies is likely to be best.

1. Use of small whiteboards and pens so that children's answers and other exploratory ideas can be written, displayed and then erased. (Some schools have technology such as voting pods or tablets linked to an interactive whiteboard which achieve similar results.) 'Show-me' techniques such as these have become particularly popular in maths lessons in recent years, some examples from that curriculum area being place-value cards, number fans, number operation cards and so on. Equivalents can be used in other curriculum areas too. You might, for example, give children cards marked from A to D for multiple choice responses to a particular set of questions, problems or challenges. These techniques have the advantage of letting you know what a range of children are thinking, rather than just the child who is selected to answer in the 'hands-up' system.
2. Writing every child's name on a card and drawing out a name at random when an answer is needed. This technique has the advantage that children's turns all come around periodically. You can increase the likelihood of this by not replacing names in the pack once drawn out. If you do this too often, though, you may lose the attention of the earliest children to be picked.
3. Making fun selections by saying something like: 'I'll take an answer from someone... whose birthday is in June/who supports Football Club X/whose first initial is between A and G, etc'. You need to know your class well before adopting this third approach and you should take care that criteria are not problematic or unduly sensitive but, like 2. above, it will allow you to randomise the responses you select.

REFLECTIVE TASK

Think about your response to children's answers. Does your current teaching style match any of the portraits below?

Teacher A is very keen to hear a particular answer to each of his questions. He is determined not to allow his lesson to be thrown off course by answers which will divert the class from the direction he has set. He dismisses answers which are not the ones he is looking for with responses like 'No, that's not it' or 'Anyone else?'

Teacher B takes up and pursues most of the answers her children offer and she takes pride in how much she values their contributions. There is a lack of direction in her lessons as she zig-zags her way through a series of disconnected responses.

Teacher C is complimentary in the extreme and praises every response a child gives with words like 'Wonderful!' and 'Excellent!'

Did you recognise any of your own classroom habits as you considered these portraits? They are a little caricatured but the features highlighted are common and demonstrate that there are a variety of ways in which this aspect of class management can be mishandled.

So what are the problems with each of these styles? You probably recognised immediately that Teacher A has too narrow a view about the sorts of answers he should allow. He pays no respect to children's answers unless they are in his script and the children will quickly become disaffected in his lessons. Questions in Teacher A's class are rather formulaic and his children are unlikely to feel that they are taking part in a dialogue during his lessons. The problems with the styles of Teacher B and Teacher C are harder to spot since both are clearly much keener to recognise and value the responses their children give and their styles therefore seem to embody some of the core values of dialogic teaching. Unfortunately these good intentions are insufficient on their own and the children in both of these classes are likely to feel frustrated (in Teacher B's class) by the lack of direction or patronised (in Teacher C's class) by praise which is given so indiscriminately that it ceases to have value.

Let us turn these observations into advice for you in your classroom.

- You should of course allow and encourage children's responses and recognise that many of them will be completely unexpected. (It is often useful to remind yourself that they have not read your lesson plan.) We can never predict with certainty the responses of any group of children or adults and sometimes an 'off-the-wall' comment or answer can bring a class to life, if handled appropriately.
- Remember, though, that the responsibility for steering the dialogue in the lesson is largely yours. Children cannot be expected to keep time or to keep their contributions moving in the direction that you have planned. Teacher A was so keen to maintain this power that he did not allow any response that he had not anticipated. Teacher B, though, allows so many responses to be aired and followed that she has effectively sacrificed any hope of keeping the lesson moving in a satisfactory direction. Although good communication in a classroom can feel like a conversation, a lesson as a whole is very different from an everyday conversation in which the participants can negotiate the direction from moment to moment. You will therefore need to decide which avenues suggested by children can be explored and which should be avoided, at least during the lesson in which they arise. Deal with the latter sensitively, 'That's an interesting point, Jack, and perhaps we can come back to it in another lesson. For now, though, I want us to follow up Rashida's point.' In the same way that you should respect children's contributions to the lesson, they should, and generally will, respect yours which, despite everything that has been said here about power-sharing, includes your right as the teacher to decide on the pace and direction of the lesson.
- Children's responses should always be treated with courtesy and respect and with an appropriate level of appreciation. It is impossible to specify what 'appropriate' will look like in every situation and you must develop your own style in the particular contexts in which you work. Some general guidance may be useful though. All children need praise and encouragement and, sadly, some do not get enough of these, either outside or inside school, but it is easy for teachers to overcompensate for this and hence to devalue the currency of their praise. Children are astute judges of sincerity. Try to avoid the extremes of either never praising or over-praising so that children can come to trust you, to recognise that you value what they say and to know that when you praise their efforts, you really mean it. A further point to make here is that you can show that you like and value children's company in the classroom in many ways. As well as praising them for the quality of their work, remember that this should not be judged against a universal standard. A creditworthy standard of work by one of your children, for example, might be a mediocre or half-hearted standard for another. Knowing your children and their capabilities is crucial since this allows you to give realistic feedback which should sometimes, though not always, include praise. You should also try to comment favourably upon your children's attitudes to their work and to the care and consideration they show towards others in the class and school community.

As we move towards the conclusion of this section, remember what was said at the beginning of this chapter about the mixture of styles that comprise dialogic teaching. The message here is a subtle one. There is a place for authoritative, teacher-directed communication alongside more open dialogue with children. (Notice the difference between the words 'authoritative' and 'authoritarian'.) Phil Scott (2008) describes an extremely useful way of looking at this in the context of science lessons. Scott suggests that communication can be analysed on two different dimensions. One dimension specifies whether the communication is *dialogic* or *authoritative* while the other specifies whether it is *interactive* or *non-interactive*. We might easily imagine that an approach that was authoritative and non-interactive would be a poor teaching style and one that ran counter to the principles of dialogic teaching but this would be a mistake. Scott's analysis reminds us that we should choose the style we use according to the needs of the children in that situation. In a science lesson there will certainly be the need for children to have the chance to explore their current ideas and to exchange these freely. There will also be the need, however, for the teacher to introduce a more expert interpretation of the situation to help the children move on in their learning. (Remember the ideas of Vygotsky and others which were considered in Chapter 3.) Scott gives the example of how *everyday* and *scientific* views differ when children consider the topic of *forces*. If the children had no input other than their own ideas they would struggle to discover the science that underlies apparently straightforward phenomena like how a bottle stays on a shelf or why a ball falls to the ground. The skill of the successful teacher lies in scaffolding children's learning and, in the case of a science lesson, providing bridges for them to move from everyday to scientific understanding (Scott, 2008). Similar needs occur elsewhere in the curriculum.

Something should be said here about listening, the mirror of talk. Clearly, for talk to be effective, there is a need for good listening and educationalists often refer to 'listening skills'. However, as with talking skills and thinking skills, it is not quite as clear what we mean by this as the words might suggest. This issue was raised in Chapter 2 and, while the use of the word skill when applied to talking, thinking, listening and so on does seem entirely legitimate, caution about these matters is never a bad thing and leads us towards greater clarity. We might, then, be specifying the behaviours that a good listener displays when we refer to listening skills, but we are all familiar with situations where this behaviour has become separated from what we understand by listening. Children who simulate good listening as a cover for a lack of attention to the speaker – a phenomenon to be found in every classroom at one time or another – for example, or, by contrast, children who stare at a television screen for the whole time that they are being spoken to but who can afterwards recount every word that has been said to them. Clearly, therefore, we do not want the surface appearances of listening on their own. Although behaviour can be a useful cue, therefore, we need to direct children's attention to the inner processes that underlie this behaviour, processes which involve thinking.

A useful distinction, which most children can eventually appreciate, is between simply hearing and listening. As I write these words, I can hear traffic and a power tool somewhere near my house. Occasionally an aircraft passes overhead. It is only when I consciously shift my attention to these sounds and listen actively to them, though, that they cease to be sounds that I hear, almost subconsciously, and become the objects of my listening. There are some excellent materials by Mercer, Dawes and Wegerif which can be used to help children develop skills in these areas (Mercer *et al.*, 2004). Listening, then, like looking (which pairs with seeing in a similar way to listening/hearing), is a matter of shifting our attention.

Bloom's taxonomy: a model to develop higher-level thinking

Working on the issues raised so far in this chapter should help you to adjust the conditions for talk in your classroom so that children can participate in a less inhibited way and feel that their contributions are valued. You can then begin to work on the tasks that you set children in order to adjust the cognitive level that these require of them. A very useful model for judging the cognitive level of tasks has been drawn from the work of educational psychologist Benjamin Bloom. Bloom argued many years ago that cognitive tasks like identification and recall were low level by comparison to tasks that required students to demonstrate understanding. Higher still in Bloom's Taxonomy of Educational Objectives were tasks like application and analysis and the highest-level tasks involved synthesis and evaluation. Bloom's Taxonomy is outlined briefly below, with lower-level tasks at the bottom of the list and with some examples to illustrate each of the six major classes. (Many more are given in the original versions of Bloom's work and in the work of subsequent writers using Bloom's Taxonomy.)

- Evaluation: *appraise, compare and contrast, judge, give arguments for and against, assess;*
- Synthesis: *bring ideas together, build upon, reorganise, combine, join up ideas;*
- Analysis: *classify, suggest reasons for, investigate;*
- Application: *use, apply, manipulate, transfer;*
- Comprehension: *understand, interpret, explain, define;*
- Knowledge: *recall, label, identify, name.*

(Based on Bloom, 1956)

PRACTICAL TASK PRACTICAL TASK **PRACTICAL TASK** PRACTICAL TASK **PRACTICAL TASK**

Make five copies of this list and use one each day for a week while you are in a teaching role. Try each day to identify some examples of questions you have asked or tasks you have set children which encourage thinking at various stages in Bloom's Taxonomy. Do not attempt to cover every possibility and be aware that there has been some dispute over the years about the levels assigned to particular tasks. (To explain something as a teacher, for example, might be regarded as a higher-order task than Bloom's Taxonomy suggests.) Try to ensure, though, that there are some opportunities for children to develop higher-level cognitive skills as well as those from lower in the list. Do you notice a tendency to ask mainly recall questions or do some tasks require evaluation or synthesis, for example? You will have to adapt this exercise to suit the situation you are in, taking account of the age of the children you are working with, but you should find that this reflection sharpens up your interactions with children and makes you more aware of opportunities that exist to raise the cognitive level of both planned and impromptu activities and interactions in your classroom. Hopefully, your lists showed more evidence of higher-order thinking as the week progressed.

Developing talk in groups

As we noted in Chapter 3, classroom researchers have known for some time that simply putting children into groups does not ensure that they will work as groups. Fortunately, however, there are approaches you can adopt which can lead to children working collaboratively and co-operatively. Valerie Coultas (2007) describes a wide range of approaches to oracy which can be used in (as her title puts it) *challenging classrooms* and across every school age range. She describes the challenge posed by group work extremely well.

> *Group work can be a frightening concept for some teachers. They may see it as an opportunity for pupils to get out of control, talk off task and generally muck about. If the group task does not really require group work this can be the result. The key test for a group task is that the group has to cooperate: the task* must *involve a group decision, negotiation or consensus of some kind, and have a real purpose.*
>
> (Coultas, 2007, p 53; author's emphasis)

At this point I should make an important point about some of the classroom approaches which we will consider in the chapters to come. To understand any of these approaches thoroughly and fully integrate them into your classroom teaching, you should attempt to obtain some further training by specialists in this area, since a book like this one can only offer a brief introduction. If attending training is not a practical option for you, you should read as many printed and online resources as you can, again taking care to select reputable sources. At the end of this chapter and the ones that follow, some links will be offered so that you can follow up the approaches which most appeal to you at present. Having said all of this, the introduction that follows should give you a good idea of what these approaches entail and a few practical ways that they can help you in the development of talk and co-operative learning in your classroom.

Collaborative learning

In Chapter 3 we saw how the *Bullock Report* (DES, 1975) had helped teachers recognise that oracy was inextricably linked to literacy – one could not develop without the other. From that time onward, approaches have been developed which have treated language development holistically. Some good examples are those which can be used in the teaching of reading and these have been used effectively in classrooms in the decades since Bullock. Some examples are cloze, sequencing and group prediction techniques which require children to work together in pairs or groups to solve a problem involving text which is in some way incomplete. Sequencing and group prediction require children to reassemble sentences from a text into the correct sequence (sequencing) or to predict what will happen next as short extracts from a story are presented to them (group prediction). You may not have come across the word 'cloze' before but this is another common and extremely useful technique involving the systematic omission of words from a text. Here is an example of a cloze text.

> Darren was unhappy that morning. It was his birthday and he had already had his presents from his mum and his sister but there was no sign of a present from his dad. Not even a card. As he got ready for school he looked down the ____ for the postman. All he could see though ____ a few cars, one or two tired-looking people ____ off to work and the bus that chugged its way through the ____. Then, as he was eating his cereal in front of the ____, Darren heard the click of the gate and the ____ of heavy footsteps as the postman came along the ____. After a few moments he heard the sound of mail being stuffed ____ the letter-box and the snapping shut of the flap. ____ was almost quick enough to catch the mail before it ____ the floor and he flicked through the envelopes ____. A gas bill, a couple of those glossy leaflets ____ bank and phone companies sent and a ____ for his mum wrapped in plastic. He threw them ____ the mat and walked sadly away.

As you can see, words have been omitted and the children's task is to decide on words which would be suitable to fill the gaps. The first couple of sentences are left intact to allow children to get a sense of what the passage is about and then words are deleted regularly. In this case the gaps are about every ten words but this pattern has been modified a little to allow a variety of words to be omitted. The intervals between gaps can be adjusted, as can the reading level required and the difficulty of the text in terms of style and subject matter. (David Wray's book in the *Learning Matters* series (Wray, 2006) will tell you more about these approaches.)

There are two important points which should be made about these kinds of approaches. The first is that the process is far more important than the product, a distinction made in Chapter 2. You should therefore be much happier with a well-argued case for a word which is not the missing word from the original text than with a quickly decided correct answer. In the example above, children might quite justifiably argue for different words to describe how Darren flicked through the envelopes: eagerly perhaps (which was the word in the original text) or anxiously, even angrily. (Notice that children will probably bring their own emotional experiences and reactions to the discussion.) The value of the exercise lies entirely in the process of articulating reasons why some words would fit while others would not. Notice, too, the gains in terms of children's grammatical understanding. The recognition that an adverb is required to fill this gap is likely to emerge much more powerfully through such discussion than it might from an exercise in a grammar lesson which offered only a decontextualised definition.

The second point to be made is that these techniques involve children in talking and thinking through discussion and such discussion is one of the elements which you need to develop in order to make your teaching more dialogic. If activities such as these are successful, children will have collaborated with one another in the process of completing them. It is possible for children to attempt such activities alone and at times this will be appropriate. If they are never offered as pair or group activities, though, then valuable opportunities for collaborative learning will be lost. For further ideas and resources you should visit the Collaborative Learning Project website (see page 68). This project is an extremely useful point of contact for any teachers wishing to pursue this kind of work. Set up by English teaching specialists with a commitment to the development of oracy, the project website contains a great deal of useful information and downloadable resources relating to various age groups and curriculum areas and, at the time of writing, access to these resources is free of charge.

Kagan structures

During the 1970s, an American educationalist named Spencer Kagan recognised the difficulty that researchers have consistently found with group work, the difficulty which Valerie Coultas described very well in the quotation on page 60. Kagan decided that children needed structures to encourage them to co-operate. The development of these 'Kagan structures', as they are known, has become a worldwide educational project and significant numbers of schools in this country now adopt these approaches. Kagan structures are all designed to create the conditions which will encourage co-operative learning and they incorporate four principles which Kagan describes as: *Positive Interdependence*, *Individual Accountability*, *Equal Participation* and *Simultaneous Interaction* (Kagan, 1994). (You might usefully consider whether authors are likely to mean the same thing, or something slightly different, when they refer to 'co-operative' as opposed to 'collaborative' learning.)

Kagan structures are content-free and can be used with the whole class, pairs (we will look at some examples of these later) or groups and, when working in groups, Kagan recommends that, where possible, four children should work together. (When class teachers or whole schools follow Kagan structures in a comprehensive way they will usually adopt his recommendations about the make-up of these groups, which are carefully constructed to mix abilities. There is insufficient space here to explore the rationale for this but it is worth noting the importance attached to inclusion in the Kagan approach.)

A useful example of a Kagan structure for use with groups is called *Numbered Heads Together*. A group talks about a particular problem, question or task and feeds back its collective response to the rest of the class. Here, however, a very useful device is used to maximise the chances of interdependence and accountability among group members. The device is to ask group members to number themselves from 1 to 4 and then a child is selected to feed back to the larger group, using a randomly generated number (using a spinner, adjusted die or computer program, for example). Returning to Kagan's principles, every child remains accountable, all participate equally and there is an interdependence among all of the group members and among the groups in the class. What this device counters is the tendency for some group members to sit back and disengage from the group activity, through shyness or apathy, for example, and for others to push themselves forward or to be selected by the teacher disproportionately often (as we considered earlier in this chapter). If children know that they may have to feed back on behalf of the group, their involvement in the group task is likely to be high: there is therefore a much greater chance of genuinely co-operative learning. Try this approach as an alternative to self-selected spokespersons in groups and you should see a noticeable difference in engagement. We will return to Kagan structures later in this chapter and in Chapter 8.

CLASSROOM STORY

A highly experienced teacher has seen very significant improvements in her teaching and her children's learning since she began to use Kagan approaches. The content-free nature of Kagan structures allows her to use them across the curriculum and in helping her mixed-ability groups to build a sense of identity and belonging. She has also found that putting children into groups of four facilitates talk since (using Kagan terminology) the children can talk to their *shoulder partners* (the child beside them) or their *face partners* (the child opposite).

Other group approaches

There are a wide range of other techniques and approaches to group work which you might also consider. Making radio programmes (as mentioned in Chapter 3 and clearly on a non-professional scale) can be a useful way of helping children to focus upon an audience (this could be another class or year group) and making a very short news, documentary or entertainment programme for them. Television programmes offer similar opportunities. If circumstances require a more easily managed activity, however, the larger scale of television programmes can, at times, be harder to handle and the sound-only nature of the radio broadcast creates more of a focus on talk.

A range of useful techniques are gathered together in the Primary National Strategies materials *Speaking, Listening, Learning: working with children in Key Stages 1 and 2* (see page 69 for the website address from which you can download these materials). Two very useful examples follow.

Jigsaw games

These activities involve children rotating around the classroom as experts from their original groups and sharing their expertise with other groups, and generally rejoining the original groups at the end. (Valerie Coultas (2007) describes this activity). So, for example, five or six groups at the beginning of this activity might each focus on one character from a story and become the 'experts' about this character. Then, through a series of group reorganisations, they share their expertise with others in order to complete a task which requires all of this expertise. (Many schools use a related, drama-based approach called *The mantle of the expert:* see page 69 for website details.)

Statements game

This activity requires children to rank a set of statements in order of importance and to place them on a triangle or diamond as shown below. The more important the statement is judged to be, the closer to the apex of the triangle or diamond it will be placed. An example might be a set of statements giving reasons for having laws.

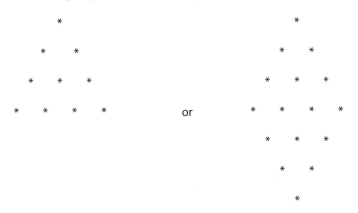

As with any activity of this kind, a focus on the justification of children's choices, in the debriefing session, is likely to improve the level of their thinking. Debriefing is another example of metacognition.

PRACTICAL TASK PRACTICAL TASK **PRACTICAL TASK** PRACTICAL TASK **PRACTICAL TASK**

The following activity will allow you to investigate the valuable resources on the Collaborative Learning Project website (see page 68 for web address) and to practise using the Kagan structure Numbered Heads Together. It will also allow you to see whether your interactions with your class have improved since the analysis you made at the beginning of this chapter.

Go onto the Collaborative Learning Project website and find a group activity to suit the age group of a class you are working with. Download the relevant resources and plan a lesson or a series of lessons in which to embed the activity. As an example you can think about how you could use the activity connected to T S Eliot's poem 'Macavity – the Mystery Cat', an activity which is probably most suitable for children aged seven or eight. Use the Kagan technique of Numbered Heads Together to choose a spokesperson from each group to justify their reasons for their decisions. (Tip: if you use a spinner or other device to choose a number, do this each time a group reports back not just once at the beginning.)

Use this example as a guide to structure the activity you use. There are many examples so choose one you feel comfortable with. Ask the children to undertake these activities in groups of four (clearly you will need to have one or two groups of three or five unless your class size is a multiple of four).

Note how the children responded to these activities. Did all of them participate at every stage? Was there evidence of higher-order thinking in the children's contributions? (When evaluating this, think of words from Bloom's Taxonomy like: *compare and contrast, judge, give arguments for and against; bring ideas together, build upon, reorganise*.)

Working in pairs

Pairs are very powerful units for talking and thinking. They offer children the security of talking time with just one other person, rather than the more daunting challenge (for many children) of speaking aloud in a group or in the whole class. They also offer a great deal of time for each child because of what Kagan calls *Equal Participation* and *Simultaneous Interaction*. These are very important points to recognise. Imagine a two-minute section of your lesson in which (rather unusually) two children talked, one after the other, for a minute each. Two children out of perhaps thirty would have had this opportunity. Now imagine the situation restructured so that the children worked in pairs. Using a Kagan structure called a *Timed Pair Share* (Kagan, 1994 and 2009), each child could have one minute of speaking time and one minute of listening time and at the end of two minutes all thirty children would have had these opportunities, rather than just two.

Asking children to work in pairs in this way is not just a Kagan approach but is now common practice in many classrooms. A term that you will often hear is 'talk partners' (although other phrases are in use) and you may have already encountered this arrangement in a classroom you have worked in. It is an approach that can be used in many curriculum areas. Kagan structures can be used to make these paired sessions more productive. For example, another Kagan structure for use with pairs is the *Rally Robin* (Kagan, 1994). 'Robin' in Kagan terminology indicates a talking activity (think of a chattering robin) and 'Rally' here conjures up the image of a rally in tennis when the ball rapidly passes from one participant to the other. In a Timed Pair Share, each participant has a designated time, say a minute, to talk without interruption and this will be appropriate when lengthy reflection or analysis is required (for example, 'In the Timed Pair Share talk to your partner, for one minute each, about the things that you learned during our visit to the old mill yesterday.') A Rally Robin is better suited to quick exchanges of information (for example, 'With your partner in this Rally Robin, try to think of as many ways that we use plastic as you can. You have one minute.') Spencer Kagan describes the ways in which the Rally Robin structure can be used with different age groups.

> *Younger students might do a RallyRobin to name colors or to create or devise possible alternative endings to a story. Older students might RallyRobin prime numbers, inert elements, possible causes or consequences of an historical event, or literary techniques. Because, like all Kagan Structures, RallyRobin is content free, it is used at all grades with a very wide range of academic content.*
>
> (Kagan, 2009, p3)

Pairs can be joined together to form groups of various sizes and this can offer children the opportunity to pool the information they have acquired at each stage of an activity, with further opportunities to negotiate the nature of this information and to prioritise its importance. If children are using the Kagan Timed Pair Share or Rally Robin pairings, they could then be combined into groups of four for Numbered Heads Together. The Primary National Strategy materials, mentioned earlier, describe groupings called 'Think-Pair-Share' which work on the same principle and the activity known as 'Snowballing' which progressively combines pairs into fours, eights and so on until the whole class is involved.

You should note that using any of these strategies once only will probably lead to little benefit. Like all of us, children need time to get used to new routines so build them in regularly and monitor the results which, hopefully, will be impressive.

Drama and role play

Drama is a subject which is harder to pigeon-hole in the primary curriculum than, say, science or PE. It is closely associated with English but it can also be used to support learning across the curriculum. Another complication is that the word 'drama' can suggest large-scale productions, either in or out of school, and much smaller, classroom-based activities. The former clearly has a great deal to offer children but it is essentially the latter which we are concerned with here.

There are a wide range of drama and role-play techniques which you can use to develop children's talk. Used regularly and matched to your curricular objectives, these can help children to become more confident and to make increasingly appropriate judgements about the audience for, and the purpose of, such communication. They can also encourage them to use their imaginations to explore issues and themes arising from the subjects and topics they study.

One common and very effective example is a role-play technique called 'hot-seating'. This involves a child, yourself or another adult playing the part of a character who is central to whatever curriculum area you are involved with at the time. It may be a historical or a fictional character, but whoever is playing that character should be able to answer questions plausibly in role. These questions, asked by children in the class, can afford deeper insights into the character's emotions and motivations. Clearly, as in all unscripted drama, the responses will be improvised but you should try to steer both questions and answers to be as evidence-based as possible.

Related to hot-seating is the 'freeze frame' technique which involves groups of children becoming silent and still (as the name of the technique suggests) while representing critical moments in any event – real or fictitious – that your class is studying. Like hot-seating, the freeze frames should be evidence-based. In the debriefing session after these representations, children can explore the inner reality of the event as experienced by the characters they modelled. A variation on freeze framing is to ask for 'photographs' of these events – an old camera can be a very useful prop for you to wield. In the debriefing session, a photograph album or slide show can be shown. It is surprising how much thinking, memory and emotion can be contained kinaesthetically through the use of such techniques. Freeze frames, hot-seating and a range of other approaches of this kind are featured in the Primary National Strategy materials (see page 69).

Teaching bilingual children

Many classrooms include bilingual children who speak English as an Additional Language (EAL) and it is important to consider the special attention to language development which these children need. The Nuffield Languages Inquiry (2000) strongly suggests, however, that we can easily underestimate the language resources which bilingual children and adults possess and we should therefore avoid taking a deficit view of their abilities. A good way of exploring this topic is to consider another important aspect of language use which is its functional nature. Language is often designed to make something happen in the world. A useful term introduced by philosophers some decades ago to describe this is 'speech act' (see, for example, Austin, 1962). In order to understand what is meant by this term, consider the use of the words 'It's cold in here'. While someone might say these words on entering a room simply as a comment on the temperature, they would often be used as an indirect request for someone else to turn up the heating or to close some windows. Similarly, to answer the question 'Have you got the time?' with 'Yes, thanks' would be thought rather cheeky. Words like this are potentially rather ambiguous and confusing unless you are a very competent speaker of English.

A less proficient user of English might understand the literal meaning of words but miss the speaker's real intention in saying them. An important implication of this for the teacher working with bilingual children is to be careful not to use too much idiomatic and indirect language when this might not be understood. Bilingual children can become quite mystified by expressions like 'What are you up to?' or 'What was the writer trying to get across?'. (Indeed, some speakers of English as a first language might find language like this harder to understand than you might imagine.) You should not attempt to simplify your language to the point that all of its richness and word play is lost since, as we have already noted, your language is an important model and reference point for children. You should, however, monitor your use of language and try to make sure that it is intelligible to as many children as possible.

All teachers have to develop the ability to switch registers, or ways of speaking, in order to communicate in particular ways. Think, for example, of the differences in the ways you would speak to your class during a whole-class lesson, to the parent of a child in your class and to a colleague during a coffee break. Having bilingual children in your class can help you to do this as their linguistic needs will often be more acute than those of other children (at least initially) and their understanding of what you say might be more literal than you intend.

Bilingual children's use of English is likely to be different from that of speakers of English as a first language in two ways. The most obvious way is that they may lack some proficiency in English. We have already considered how skilled in English (or any mother tongue) children generally are, even before they reach school. If bilingual children come to this country with little or no English, or come to school having a different mother tongue to English, then they will have a great deal of skill to acquire in English in order to fully access the curriculum and to interact with their peers. The good news is that with appropriate support bilingual children can make remarkably rapid progress.

The second way in which bilingual children's language is likely to differ from that of their peers is through the influence of their mother tongue. There may be subtle difficulties that children experience in English because of the ways that English differs from their mother tongue. One example is that speakers of many languages from India, Pakistan and Bangladesh have difficulty mastering what we term the 'definite article' in English – the word 'the' – since there is no direct equivalent of this grammatical item in many of their mother tongues. It pays class teachers therefore, to have some knowledge of the mother tongues of bilingual learners in their class. Clearly this is likely to be quite limited, especially if there are a range of mother tongues spoken and if your time in the classroom is brief, but some teachers do not even know which mother tongues children in their classes speak and this is clearly an unsatisfactory state of affairs. By contrast, being able to say even the simplest phrase in a child's mother tongue is likely to be much appreciated by the child and by any family members who come to hear of this.

Community languages such as Urdu, Punjabi and other languages introduced to this country as new communities have arrived, often lack the status they deserve in the wider community. Bilingual children themselves can therefore feel that their own languages are in some way inferior to English and other European languages. Children and their families frequently have remarkable multilingual skills which can be unappreciated in school as we have already noted. Try to encourage respect for these accomplishments in your class. Making a positive feature of the enrichment which the mother tongues of bilingual learners and their families bring to your classroom makes a powerful statement of support to children who can easily feel marginalised and who can even fall victim to racism within school. The idea that one particular language is superior to others is a myth which surfaces from time to time and it is important to recognise that there is no linguistic evidence to support such claims.

Other useful strategies that you should consider when teaching bilingual learners include good use of audio-visual aids to support teaching and learning. There should be encouragement for children to contribute orally in the ways suggested in this chapter but without such contributions being forced upon bilingual children (or any children for that matter). An extended silent period, while children soak up the new language around them as they prepare to speak independently, is entirely normal and children should not be hurried into speaking before they are ready as this may jeopardise their long-term development and confidence in using English.

A final point to remember is that it is easy to underestimate bilingual children's ability and the level of work that they may be capable of. Although bilingual children will benefit from the assistance of any specialist EAL teachers and mother tongue speakers who are available, such support is often limited and the class teacher plays a key role. Try to help bilingual children overcome the language barriers they face without removing the cognitive demands in the work you set them. It should be clear from this brief review that good teaching for bilingual children is in many respects the same as good teaching for all children. If you would like more background information on these matters, you might find the work of Jim Cummins useful (for example, Cummins, 2000).

A SUMMARY OF **KEY POINTS**

> **The dialogic teaching approach advocated by Robin Alexander is an extremely useful model if you wish to make your teaching more oracy-based. Alexander suggests that dialogic teaching has five elements. Three of these – recitation, rote and instruction/exposition – are more commonly found than the other two – discussion and dialogue – and so you should work hard to develop this pair in your classroom.**

> The way in which questions and answers are handled in your classroom is crucial. You should work on techniques to improve these and examine the ethos in your classroom about who can contribute and how.

> A range of approaches to collaborative and co-operative work, based on purposeful discussion, have been considered. The Kagan approach offers many useful structures to develop co-operative learning. Focused group work is vital, as is the use of pairs such as talk partners.

> A variety of approaches from drama and role play can enhance your teaching and you should explore these with your class.

> Bilingual learners have particular needs with regard to the development of their oracy skills. A classroom which is well-run for bilingual learners is likely to be a good classroom for all children to learn in.

REFERENCES REFERENCES **REFERENCES** REFERENCES **REFERENCES** REFERENCES

Alexander, R J (2008) *Towards dialogic teaching*. (4th edition). York: Dialogos.

Askew, M and Wiliam, D (1995) *Recent research in mathematics education 5–16*. London: HMSO/OFSTED.

Austin, J L (1962) *How to do things with words*. Oxford: Clarendon Press.

Bloom, B S (1956) *Taxonomy of educational objectives. Book 1 Cognitive Domain*. New York: David McKay.

Coultas, V (2007) *Constructive talk in challenging classrooms*. Abingdon: Routledge.

Cummins, J (2000) *Language, power and pedagogy: bilingual children in the crossfire.* Clevedon: Multilingual Matters.

DES (1975) *A language for life*. London: HMSO.

Kagan, S (1994) *Cooperative Learning*. San Clemente, California: Kagan Publishing.

Kagan, S (2009) *The instructional revolution*. Kagan Publishing & Professional Development. 1(800) 933-2667 1(800) 266-7576 Accessible at: www.kaganonline.com/KaganClub/FreeArticles.html

Mercer, N and Dawes, L (2008) 'The value of exploratory talk' In Mercer, N and Hodgkinson, S (eds) *Exploring talk in school*. London: Sage.

Mercer, N, Dawes, L and Wegerif, R (2004) *Thinking together. A programme of activities for developing speaking, listening and thinking skills for children aged 8 to 11*. (2nd edition). Birmingham: Questions Publishing Company.

The Nuffield Languages Inquiry (2000) *Languages: the next generation.* London: The Nuffield Foundation.

Scott, P H (2008) Talking a way to understanding in Science classrooms, in Mercer, N and Hodgkinson, S (eds) *Exploring talk in school*. London: Sage.

Wray, D (2006) *Teaching literacy across the primary curriculum*. Exeter: Learning Matters.

Useful websites

The Collaborative Learning Project at www.collaborativelearning.org contains an extensive range of oracy-based materials which can be downloaded. Strongly linked to the Collaborative Learning Project is the London Association of Teachers of English (LATE) at www.late.org.uk. A very useful site dealing with the teaching of bilingual children is www.naldic.org.uk.

To find out more about the Kagan approach, visit www.kaganonline.com. In this country, the sole source of Kagan accredited training is Teacher to Teacher (UK) Limited and you can access their website at www.t2tuk.co.uk. Another useful site is www.Kagan-UK.co.uk.

You can download the Primary National Strategy materials *Speaking, Listening, Learning: working with children in Key Stage 1 and Key Stage 2* at:

www.nationalstrategies.standards.dcsf.gov.uk/node/84856.

You can find out more about the approach known as *The mantle of the expert* at:

www.mantleoftheexpert.com.

6
Classroom strategies to develop thinking and philosophy

Chapter objectives

By the end of this chapter you will have considered:

- how talk, thinking and philosophy relate to the Essentials for Learning and Life in the new primary curriculum;
- ways to encourage the development of children's thinking skills in your classroom;
- ways in which philosophy can help children to develop a range of thinking and interpersonal skills;
- classroom approaches to philosophy in the primary school and P4C in particular;
- other important approaches to the development of thinking, including TASC, Six Thinking Hats and Building Learning Power.

This will help you to make progress towards these Professional Standards for the award of QTS:

Q1, Q2, Q4, Q6, Q7a, Q7b, Q8, Q10, Q14, Q23, Q28, Q29, Q30, Q32

Introduction: approaches to the development of thinking skills

In this chapter we will build upon the insights and approaches introduced so far in this book as we shift the focus from the development of talk to the development of thinking. You will see, however, that we will keep returning to many of the same issues considered in connection with talk as the two are so strongly linked. In this section we will try to gain a broader view of the set of attributes that are generally referred to as 'thinking skills'.

As you will recall from Chapter 2, there are many approaches to the development of thinking skills and the relationships between them are quite complex. A group of experts in this field have analysed many such approaches in a very useful reference guide called *Frameworks for thinking* (Moseley et al., 2005). In this book the authors have evaluated and compared 41 separate approaches, an indication of just how diverse this area is. Clearly, these approaches are not entirely different from one another and part of the task the authors set themselves is to group them into broad categories (Moseley et al., 2005, p6). Two of the authors of this book, Steve Higgins and Jennifer Miller, have produced a separate classification of approaches to thinking skills as part of a resource database which, at the time of writing, is located on the DCSF Standards Site website (website address given on page 88). Both book and website are likely to be valuable to anyone wishing to gain a broader view of this field and are recommended as reference guides. *Frameworks for thinking*, in particular, offers very useful evaluations of the approaches considered. They are such extensive resources, however, that using them as a basis for selecting approaches for your own classroom context could be difficult. Another difficulty is that any categorisation of approaches draws our attention, quite naturally, to the differences between approaches rather than to their similarities. The DCSF Standards Site website employs the image of a Venn diagram, which is helpful in reminding us that most approaches of this kind have features in common.

In this chapter and in Chapter 7 we will examine a much smaller number of approaches which aim to help children become better thinkers. They are different but compatible and can therefore work well together to achieve different objectives. It is important, though, to be careful about your selection. Different approaches and combinations will work well in different settings but there is certainly no suggestion that you try to adopt all of the approaches which will be considered. We will return to this issue of blending approaches across the classroom and school in Chapter 8.

Another important question which often arises in connection with thinking skills is whether they are best taught separately or through other curriculum areas. It is better not to regard these options as mutually exclusive but to adopt a mixed approach including all of the following:

1. regular sessions which are aimed primarily at the development of thinking skills without necessarily being linked to particular curriculum areas;
2. teaching thinking skills through the subjects or areas of learning in the curriculum – this can be subdivided into:
    a) specific opportunities to encourage thinking skills which can be found in the contexts provided by particular subjects;
    b) adjustments and additions to your regular teaching designed to exploit opportunities for developing thinking skills.

In this chapter we will concentrate on approaches related to 1. above and in Chapter 7 we will examine approaches related to 2.

The advice which was given earlier should be repeated here. From this book you should gain a good understanding of the basic principles of these approaches (although the level of detail given about each one will vary) and you should be able to implement some of these approaches in your own classroom. However, your expertise will be boosted enormously by further reading and, better still, by expert training in the areas you most wish to develop. The apparent simplicity of each of these approaches conceals sophisticated theoretical foundations and to simply copy a procedure that you have seen or read about will not give you the insights that you need to develop your skills fully. We will return to the benefits of training and development in a whole-school context in Chapter 8.

What do we mean by thinking skills?

At this point we should consider the most fundamental question we could ask about thinking skills: does it even make sense to describe thinking as a set of skills? To help us deal with this question, it may be helpful to consider the analogy of another area in which skills can (at first sight at least) be identified less problematically. Let us consider, therefore, the skills involved in driving.

To identify the skills of driving we might begin with the set of physical actions required, such as steering, accelerating, braking and gear changing. Closer consideration of any one of these in operation on the road, however, reveals a complex web of skills, awareness and understanding involved in its execution. Steering, for example, requires the physical ability to hold the car on a straight or curved path. Almost beyond our awareness, though, this action in practice also depends upon a feedback loop involving our response to what we see, hear and feel as each sense gives us fresh information about the performance of the car and the road ahead. Often, too, broad physical skills of this kind must be used in combination with one another and with the less obvious cognitive and emotional responses which accompany them. (Think, for example, of all of the responses that might arise while driving along an icy road.) It is the ability to effectively use this large range of skills over a sustained period of time which allows us to claim, with confidence, that a person is a good driver but it is clear that these skills include what we might call 'dispositions' (for example, alertness, careful judgement, care for others) as well as the more obvious physical skills required to keep the car in motion. In fact, the latter without the former has the potential to be extremely dangerous, as we regularly see in the cases of drunken drivers and so-called joyriders.

Returning then to thinking skills, we have similar difficulties when we try to pin down exactly what we mean by that phrase. In this chapter we will consider two ways of viewing children and thinking skills: first, the picture that emerges from key documentation and, later in the chapter, a more holistic view focusing on the children who exemplify these skills.

How are talk and thinking skills defined in the new primary curriculum?

Although this chapter is concerned primarily with thinking and philosophy, it seems more sensible to look at talk too when we consider the new primary curriculum. The new primary curriculum has two organisational structures which you will use together in planning and teaching lessons. The two structures are called Areas of Learning – these replace the 'subjects' in the current National Curriculum – and Essentials for Learning and Life – these are the skills which will be developed at the same time as the Areas of Learning. In this chapter we will look at the Essentials for Learning and Life and in the next chapter at the Areas of Learning. The six elements of Essentials for Learning and Life are as follows:

- Literacy;
- Numeracy;
- ICT capability;
- Learning and thinking skills;
- Personal and emotional skills;
- Social skills.

For all references to the new primary curriculum, go to the website address which was given on page 5.

To some extent, all six elements are relevant to the development of talk, thinking and philosophy. Most relevant are Learning and thinking skills and Literacy but there is a substantial overlap, too, with Personal and emotional skills and with Social skills. Let us look at the two most relevant categories in more detail.

Learning and thinking skills

Focus: *Children have the skills to learn effectively. They can plan, research and critically evaluate, using reasoned arguments to support conclusions. They think creatively, making original connections and generating ideas. They consider alternative solutions to problems.*

Children learn how to:

1. investigate, *asking relevant questions, identifying problems, analysing and judging the value of information and ideas, questioning assumptions. They plan systematically using time and resources effectively, anticipating, taking and managing risks;*

2. create and develop, *using their imagination to explore possibilities and generate ideas. They try out innovative alternatives, looking for patterns, recognising differences and making generalisations, predicting outcomes and making reasoned decisions;*

3. communicate, *interacting with different audiences in a variety of ways using a range of media;*

4. evaluate, *developing criteria for judging work and suggesting refinements and improvements.*

(http://curriculum.qcda.gov.uk/new-primary-curriculum/essentials-for-learning-and-life/
learning-and-thinking-skills/index.aspx)

If we look at Literacy, we can see that some elements of 'talk' are subsumed within it but, as we shall see in Chapter 7, a substantial amount of guidance is also given in the Area of Learning called Understanding English, communication and languages. We will therefore, have a better picture of the requirements for talk when we consider that Area of Learning but you should be able to see elements too in the description of Literacy below.

Literacy

Focus: *Children use and apply their literacy skills confidently and competently in their learning and in everyday contexts. They convey ideas and opinions clearly, and respond creatively and critically to a wide range of information and ideas.*

Children learn how to:

1. listen attentively, *talk clearly and confidently about their thoughts, opinions and ideas, listening carefully to others so that they can refine their thinking and express themselves effectively;*

2. read accurately *and fluently to comprehend and critically respond to texts of all kinds, on paper and on screen, in order to access ideas and information;*

3. write, present and broadcast *a range of ideas, in a wide variety of forms and with awareness of different audiences and purposes; communicate these ideas with accuracy on paper, on screen and through multimodal texts;*

4. analyse, evaluate and criticise *a range of uses of language in order to draw out meaning, purpose and effect.*

(http://curriculum.qcda.gov.uk/new-primary-curriculum/essentials-for-learning-and-life/
literacy/index.aspx)

In the next part of this chapter we will consider a number of approaches to the development of thinking skills beginning with P4C. To understand that approach fully, however, we must first consider the wider issue of the benefits which philosophy can bring to both children and adults.

The value of philosophy in the classroom

It is worth reminding ourselves that, while terms like 'thinking skills' (and other related terms such as 'critical thinking' and 'creative thinking') are relatively new to the classroom, philosophy has been practised and studied in the West for more than two and a half millennia. You may have preconceptions of philosophy which are somewhat negative. Philosophers are often pictured as remote, unemotional characters (and generally as old, white men) who spend their days pondering problems that others would regard as trivial or pointless. The following famous example of a philosophical problem captures this quite well.

REFLECTIVE TASK
REFLECTIVE TASK

Read this story and try to notice your immediate reaction to it:

The ancient Chinese philosopher Zhuangzi dreamed one night that he was a butterfly and, when he awoke, he worried that he might be a butterfly dreaming that he was a Chinese philosopher.

(Adapted from the Chuang-tzu and retold often, including in Tom Stoppard's play
Rosencratz and Guildenstern are Dead)

On hearing this story, many adults (and perhaps some readers of this book) will regard the philosopher and his waking concerns as ridiculous or even irritating. Others, however, will be intrigued and will find themselves drawn into the problem that Zhuangzi's dream posed for him and the questioning of taken-for-granted aspects of everyday reality which it invites. For Zhuangzi's concern touches upon some of the most fundamental issues in philosophy, including the nature of reality itself (an area of study known to philosophers as 'metaphysics') and the nature of knowledge (the name for this area of philosophy is 'epistemology' and the area we referred to as Philosophy of Mind in Chapter 4 is generally regarded as a branch of epistemology). Far from being the sole concern of philosophy, though, these issues are explored in different ways by specialists in other fields such as cosmologists (who study the nature and origins of the universe), theologians (who study religious perspectives on reality) and by many others. There are also links with the work of poets and artists (look at the poems and paintings of William Blake, for example) and with those of mathematicians (consider, for example, the idea of infinity, an extremely important concept in mathematics). Another area of philosophy which is of great importance to people in other disciplines is ethics. The most obvious example of this is to those in the legal professions but those involved in medical issues are frequently drawn into ethical debates too. Although philosophy can seem like a specialist area, disconnected from all practical walks of life, this is far from the case and, as we shall see, children can benefit from early exploration of many philosophical issues.

Like adults, children can be intrigued and provoked into deep thought by problems like the 'butterfly dream' described above. Children generally have less rigid views than adults of the world around them and they relish stories which give an unusual perspective on everyday reality. Many of the books, TV programmes and movies that children most enjoy are based upon imaginary worlds or, perhaps more accurately, worlds similar to their own but radically altered by strange or magical interventions. A few examples from recent years are the TV series *Dr Who*, the books (and movie adaptations) of the *Harry Potter* stories, the *Lord of the Rings* trilogy, the *Narnia* series, and a myriad of myths and legends. You will probably recall here the model of child development proposed by Kieran Egan and Alison Gopnik's ideas about *counterfactual thinking* which were discussed in Chapter 4 (see pages 35–36). Their ideas are important in helping us to understand the passionate interest that children typically show in such stories. The plot lines of *Dr Who*, with their portrayal of time travel and its dilemmas, can stimulate children's thinking in the same way as the 'butterfly dream'. Some critics, though, have questioned whether this fascination for such issues and the enquiries which flow from it can justifiably be called 'philosophy'. We will explore this argument a little further in the next section.

PRACTICAL TASK PRACTICAL TASK PRACTICAL TASK PRACTICAL TASK PRACTICAL TASK

The ability to distinguish between facts and opinions is a vital one for children of any school age to develop. Dealing with this in class can be a philosophical exercise leading to an exploration of truth claims and justified or unjustified beliefs. At a less abstract level, it can help children become more discerning in their ability to sift and evaluate the information which surrounds them. (You should see links here with Bloom's Taxonomy and a number of other models covered so far in this book.)

There are many ways to set up an activity like this. Elaine Richard's useful book *10 Critical Thinking Card Games* (Richard, 2005) has a useful version of this and other activities. (The contexts used in this book are from the USA. This might be a slight, though not insurmountable, obstacle for British schoolchildren.) You can set an exercise like this up yourself in many ways. Use your imagination and think about contexts which would engage children. For example, you might ask your children to consider a set of statements about famous people, including sporting and pop stars. You might give them these statements on cards and ask them to work collaboratively to sort them into facts and opinions. Can they tell the difference, for example, between statements like 'X is 23 years old and was born in Brazil' and 'X is the best footballer in the world'?

Can children study philosophy?

As with so many interesting and important questions, the first response to be made is that it depends what we mean by the terms 'study' and 'philosophy'. At one level the answer is clearly 'Yes' since information about, for example, the history of philosophy and of some of the great philosophers and their ideas can be conveyed to children (above a certain age anyway) without undue difficulty. Whether children would necessarily find these stories engaging or relevant to their own lives and concerns is less clear and this takes us to the heart of the question. Critics such as Fox (2001) have maintained that children lack the life experiences and the intellectual maturity to address the issues of philosophy in any meaningful way. Sometimes this point of view is expressed with reference to the ideas of Piaget (which we examined in Chapter 3) or another similar developmental model.

Karin Murris has explored this issue (Murris, 2000 and 2001, the latter being a reply to Fox's objections) and she offers some very useful ways of looking at the situation. She cites the philosopher Mary Midgley who argues that:

> *Of course children's arguments are not the same as the discussions of university students. But then neither is a child's eager participation when his or her parents*

are mending the garage just like the work which the child may do later as an engineering student. In both, what matters is to pick up the general spirit of such activities, to start seeing them as interesting and possible. And if one does not do this as a child, it is much harder to do it later.

(Murris, 2000, p263)

The last sentence of this quotation is perhaps the most telling. Children may not be, and probably will not be, engaged in the more advanced and esoteric discipline of philosophy as it is taught to undergraduates, but they are engaged in comparable activities which are relevant to their own lives. These endeavours deserve to go under the name of philosophy, Murris (2000, p263) points out, as much as school mathematics and history deserve those names. Murris goes a stage further with her argument that children are well suited to philosophy. She refers to the work of Gareth Matthews (1994) and notes his suggestion *that children are the 'natural' philosophers, in contrast to adult philosophers who cultivate young children's sense of wonder* (Murris, 2000, p272). Murris goes on to explore even more fundamental questions:

Is it indeed true to say that childhood is something we leave behind, and replace by the same, albeit more mature? Or can we make a claim for the uniqueness of childhood? What exactly falls under the concept child of 'childhood'?

(Murris, 2000, p272; author's emphasis)

In other words it may be adults rather than children who lack the disposition needed to fully embrace philosophical investigation. To return to the question we considered in Chapters 2 and 3, of whether or not young children can 'decentre' from their own experiences, Matthews (1994) answers unequivocally that they can, citing a number of examples of children's philosophical questions and empathetic responses. These questions are profound and a fuller exploration of them is beyond the scope of this book. Hopefully, though, the case for children's study of topics in ways which could justifiably be called 'philosophical' has been made sufficiently well for our present purposes.

So what kinds of issues can children consider in this way? Children's life inside and outside of school constantly throws up situations which could provoke philosophical enquiry: the fairness with which items are shared, the punishments which follow unwanted behaviour (these two relate to the philosophical area of ethics, mentioned above), the wonder at a beautiful piece of music (the philosophical area of aesthetics), the sadness brought about by the death of loved ones (pets as well as humans) and so on. A wide variety of approaches can offer the opportunity to explore at least some of these issues. The advantage of a philosophical approach, however, is that it can help structure such enquiries for children and can encourage the development of logic and reasoning which are needed to pursue these and similar enquiries in a productive manner.

So far, this has been an argument for the benefits of philosophy in general but, as we have already concluded, philosophy of the exact kind studied in universities is not likely to be a good fit for the primary classroom. Some adjustment has to be made and a variety of philosophical approaches have been used in classrooms over the last few decades. In Scotland the Community of Philosophical Inquiry (CoPI) designed by Catherine McCall (2009) is an approach which strongly emphasises philosophical rigour. Another dialogue-based approach which is often used in association with Global Citizenship is Open Spaces for Dialogue in Education (OSDE). (A web address for OSDE is given on page 88.) Probably the most popular and enduring model for helping children to think in a philosophical manner in this country, though, is P4C (as some practitioners prefer the term 'Philosophy with Children' you will sometimes see it abbreviated to PwC.) Like CoPI, P4C lays a strong emphasis on the development of philosophical thinking as opposed to a more general kind of critical thinking. We will explore this approach further in the following sections.

PRACTICAL TASK PRACTICAL TASK **PRACTICAL TASK** PRACTICAL TASK **PRACTICAL TASK**

An interesting exercise is to ask children to think of 'nothing' and to describe their thoughts. This can lead them quite naturally to conclude that 'nothing' is impossible to imagine – whatever we see (blackness, an empty sky, a deserted landscape) or hear (the sound of our pulse, distant sounds of traffic and so on) are always 'something'. With older groups this can lead on to some deep philosophical thinking. David A White's book *Philosophy for Kids* (White, 2001) relates this exercise to the philosophical speculations of the ancient philosopher Parmenides who conjectured that 'nothing' might not exist at all. (This exercise with children is also described by the philosopher Peter Worley – web address on page 88.) White's book contains 40 such examples linked to the thinking of philosophers from the ancients up to the twentieth century. This book is probably most suited to pupils of secondary school age but it is a useful resource to consider using with some groups in Years 5 or 6. Thinking about 'nothing' can be undertaken by much younger children, although the discussion would be likely to have a different trajectory. A resource which might precede or follow up this discussion with children in Key Stage 1 is Mick Inkpen's lovely story *Nothing* (see page 107 for details).

P4C

P4C is practised around the world and stems from the work of an American academic philosopher named Matthew Lipman. Lipman became frustrated with his students' inability to reason and, in the late 1960s and early 1970s, he developed, with a number of collaborators, the classroom-based approach which became known as P4C. P4C uses as its main classroom structure the *community of enquiry*, the coming together of children to discuss questions that they themselves have posed. Children are helped to develop philosophical skills by a skilled facilitator – who is often their class teacher – and great emphasis is placed upon the caring dimension of such interactions. The teaching of P4C began in this country in the early 1990s, largely inspired by a BBC documentary (BBC, 1990) showing Lipman's approach in the USA, along with Catherine McCall's CoPI which was mentioned earlier. At the time of writing, more than 10,000 teachers in England and Wales have undertaken a two-day practitioner training course in P4C accredited by SAPERE, the national body for the advancement of philosophical enquiry and reflection. It is therefore an approach with a growing number of supporters. (The SAPERE website, where you can get more information about P4C, is listed on page 88.)

The community of enquiry, as employed in P4C, offers teachers and children a deceptively simple but highly effective structure through which a wide variety of issues can be explored. (The term 'community of enquiry' – sometimes spelled 'inquiry' and sometimes extended to 'philosophical inquiry' – has an interesting lineage which is unfortunately beyond the scope of this book.) I have described this structure as 'deceptively simple' because, although the setting is easy to organise in physical terms, the skills required of the facilitator are subtle and must be very well developed if the outcomes are to be successful.

The children and facilitator sit in a circle or horseshoe and to begin the enquiry (after some warm-up and settling activities) the facilitator will introduce a stimulus which may or may not have naturally arisen in the classroom. In Matthew Lipman's original structure his own materials, specifically written to provoke and develop philosophical enquiry, were used and this is still an approach taken in some places. Other writers such as Robert Fisher (1996) and Paul Cleghorn (2003) have developed materials more recently and these are certainly worth considering by practitioners. (See the next Practical Task on page 80.) Additionally, though, it has become common practice in this country for practitioners to use their own stimulus materials. These could be stories, photographs, artefacts, music, newspaper extracts or virtually anything which the facilitator feels might stimulate a good philosophical discussion.

The structure of the community of enquiry allows opportunities, through its seating and turn-taking arrangements, for points of view to be expressed and developed fairly. The community of enquiry can be run as frequently or infrequently as desired but running a minimum of one each week, with a duration of about an hour, creates the basis for continuity and progression. In the community of enquiry the children have the opportunity to devise their own questions which are then offered to the community for consideration and one question is democratically selected for discussion.

This democratic choice of question is a very significant feature and distinguishes P4C from many other discussion-based approaches in which the teacher might select the topic for discussion. The disadvantages of allowing children to set the agenda in this way are that the teacher cannot predict the direction of the enquiry (a photograph of space which the facilitator might imagine would lead to a scientific discussion could provoke a discussion about the cost of space travel or about loneliness, for example) and, as Catherine McCall points out, the facilitator cannot bring her own expertise to bear on the choice of question (McCall, 2009). In McCall's approach – CoPI – the facilitator chooses the question which appears to have the greatest philosophical potential. However, an enormous benefit which emerges from the more democratic method of question selection in P4C is that children have ownership of the questions chosen and, consequently, they will probably feel far more involved with the process than if the questions were always set by the adult in charge. This accords with a powerful and growing movement in schools to develop 'pupil voice', to which we will return in Chapter 8.

The democratic ethos of P4C enquiries relates to its attempt to develop simultaneously three different kinds of thinking. These are described by Matthew Lipman (2003) as *critical, creative* and *caring*. The democratic ethos and practices, the consideration shown to others, the care taken to establish appropriate turn-taking, all relate to caring thinking while the use of logic and intellectual rigour relate to critical thinking. All three of Lipman's thinking types are hard, and perhaps impossible, to define in such a way that we will always be able to recognise them and tell them apart from other types. Lipman and others have made extremely good attempts at this, though, and Lipman's book *Thinking in education* (Lipman, 2003) is highly recommended for any reader wishing greater insight into these distinctions. In attempting to give a brief introductory idea of the third, and most elusive, of Lipman's categories – creative thinking – it is useful to consider one of his efforts to pin this down:

> *Creative thinking is exemplified by the thinking that goes into the making of art, by the idiosyncratic encoding through which each work withholds itself from us. It is the discrimination of or the fabrication of relationships, patterns and orders producing in us the shock of unfamiliarity.*
>
> (Lipman, 2003, p248)

(It is important to point out, particularly given the focus of this book, that in this country a fourth element – collaborative thinking – is always added to the three named above and these are often referred to collectively as the 'Four Cs of P4C'.) We will return to the problematic area of creativity and creative thinking later in this chapter when we consider Edward de Bono's Six Thinking Hats and in the final two chapters.

Returning to the structure of the community of enquiry, the authors of the question chosen are generally given the opportunity to begin the discussion and then the discussion proceeds, often with speakers nominated by the speaker preceding them – another device which hands over a significant part of the teacher/facilitator's power (as opposed to the teacher's authority which is maintained throughout). You might like to contrast this with Mercer and Dawes' classroom 'rules' which were identified in the previous chapter (see page 55). At the end of an enquiry there is no intention to ensure a consensus. The intention instead is that all participants will leave the community with their own views about an issue deepened and having had the opportunity to consider it from their own perspective and from the perspective of others in the community. All of those intentions should have been realised in ways which develop participants' abilities to think about and discuss future topics in more philosophical ways.

In constructing P4C, Lipman drew from a number of roots. Within philosophy itself it is strongly influenced by the approach taken by Socrates, one of the most important of the Ancient Greek philosophers. You have probably heard something of Socrates. You might know, for example, that Socrates was a philosopher and that he died at his own hand, drinking hemlock as a death sentence passed by the Athenian authorities. His relevance to this discussion, however, is in his approach, which is still referred to as the 'Socratic method' nearly two and a half thousand years after his death. Socrates would engage in dialogue with those who raised a point of view that he wished to examine and, in answering Socrates' questions, the issue in question would become clearer. Generally those in dialogue with Socrates would be persuaded that there were weaknesses or inconsistencies in their arguments which would not have come to light without such perceptive questioning. You can find a detailed account of the Socratic method in many books and if you are particularly interested in reading more you might read Plato's accounts of Socrates' dialogues. An interesting and important point to be made is that you will only find such accounts in the writings of others – for all his importance, Socrates did not leave written records himself but operated in an entirely oral tradition which changed the course of Western culture.

P4C has also been influenced by Vygotsky's ideas about the social construction of meaning. You will recall that these ideas were explored in earlier chapters and that they are important ideas too in the rationale for dialogic teaching. There is therefore a strong connection between P4C and dialogic teaching and the two share many of the same aims. This can be seen if we compare the main features of dialogic teaching (Alexander, 2008) with some of the features of the community of enquiry (Lipman, 2003):

> *Dialogic teaching is . . . 'collective, reciprocal, supportive, cumulative and purposeful'.*
> (Alexander, 2008, p.28)

> *In a community of inquiry [Lipman's preferred spelling] the following features may be found: 'inclusiveness', 'shared cognition', 'feelings of social solidarity', 'deliberation', 'the quest for meaning'.*
> (Lipman, 2003, pp95–96)

These selections from Lipman's writing are taken from a list containing 15 features so it is clear that his ideas do not map onto Alexander's exactly, but hopefully you can see a significant overlap between the approaches that Alexander and Lipman are suggesting.

PRACTICAL TASK PRACTICAL TASK **PRACTICAL TASK** PRACTICAL TASK **PRACTICAL TASK**

A useful starting point for leading philosophical discussions is the structured material of authors like Robert Fisher and Paul Cleghorn. One example of each author's output is given in the References on page 88 but they have both produced a range of materials designed to be used in P4C settings. The two books listed are suitable for children in Key Stage 2 and give a variety of stimuli and support materials for teachers using them.

Is P4C the same as debating or circle time?

Although P4C has something in common with debating there are very important differences between the two activities. While participants in debate are generally concerned with winning an argument, beating their opponents and so on, P4C is, as we have seen, a much more collaborative approach. Good listening is as important as good speaking in P4C and the approach encourages participants to listen to the viewpoints of others with a caring, compassionate attitude. The development of emotional intelligence is given high priority in P4C, which is an excellent pedagogy to help develop this set of attributes. Lipman points out too that, in contrast to P4C, those taking part in debates *need not believe in the position they are trying to get others to accept* (Lipman, 2003, p96). Opinions may change during or following a P4C enquiry and it is important that children appreciate that any views expressed can be challenged or contested. Sincere expression of belief is, however, an important feature of P4C, rather than the adoption of intellectual positions for convenience or effect.

There are some similarities and some important differences too between P4C and the popular approach of circle time but these two approaches are again very different in at least one important respect. P4C is essentially a thinking skills programme in which, as we have seen, participants are helped to develop the tools of logic and reason needed to deal with enquiry – the tools of philosophy in fact – whereas circle time, as it is generally taught, is mainly a vehicle for helping children develop their emotional and interpersonal skills. The most obvious similarity between the two approaches is the seating arrangement which is common to circle time and the community of enquiry but they also share an ethos of caring, as was made clear above, and this makes them both highly suitable for the Essentials for Learning and Life strands described as Social skills and Personal and emotional skills.

Thinking actively in a social context (TASC)

Another very useful approach to the development of thinking skills is TASC. Developed by Belle Wallace (for example, Wallace 2002) this approach offers children a different set of tools to P4C but the two approaches coincide in many of their aims. While P4C is primarily concerned with setting up situations to facilitate philosophical enquiry, TASC helps children to tackle problems and projects that arise across the curriculum in a systematic way.

An image which is of great importance in TASC is the TASC Wheel (sometimes known as the TASC Problem-Solving Wheel), shown on page 81. The eight stages shown in the segments of the wheel represent the common elements of the process which most projects from

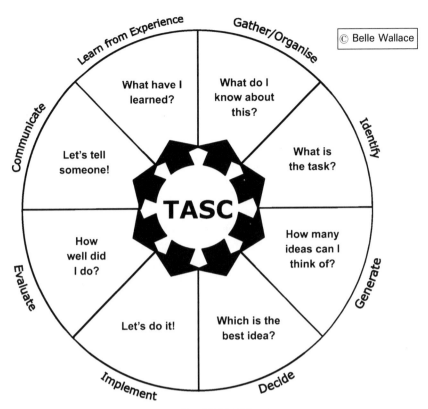

Figure 6.1. The TASC Wheel

across the curriculum require children to undertake. Beginning in the top right segment ('Gather/Organise'), the steps are labelled with descriptive terms – 'Identify', 'Learn from Experience', etc. – and each is accompanied by a corresponding question in child-friendly language which can be posed by children and teachers to begin that stage of the process. It is therefore straightforward for both teachers and children and the eight steps follow a sequence summed up in the popular phrase 'Plan, Do and Review'. (Copies of the wheel and other resources can be obtained via the TASC Wheel website, details of which are given on page 88.) Although the eight stages form a coherent and comprehensive sequence, the process does not have to be followed rigidly. Steps may be missed out and intuitive paths through the process are encouraged. TASC aims to promote creativity of thought and outcome. Great emphasis is also placed upon helping children to relax in order to maximise their learning potential. (You should recall here the neuroscientific evidence supporting this strategy that we considered in Chapter 4.)

Like P4C, TASC is a pedagogical model which owes a great deal to the theories of Vygotsky. The phrase 'social context' in its name gives a strong clue about the importance of this element. It is in fact similar to P4C in a number of ways.

- Both approaches see constructive talk as central to learning.
- Each approach has the central aim of helping children to develop social and interpersonal skills. Wallace uses the paired terms 'human' and 'humane' in a way which has some echoes of the distinction made in P4C between 'able to reason' and 'reasonable'.
- Both approaches are explicitly designed to encourage metacognition.

At this point, it is important for you to understand a little more about metacognition, a term which has been used a number of times up to this point. The term was introduced by Flavell in 1976 to describe *one's knowledge concerning one's own cognitive processes or anything related to them* (Flavell, 1976, p232). As we noted in Chapter 2, metacognition has been identified as being crucial to the development of thinking and correlates with educational success more generally (Hattie, 2008). Many approaches to learning encourage metacognition, not just those specifically targeted at the development of thinking skills. As we saw, too, there are very strong links between what we understand by metacognition and the crucial group of attributes labelled 'executive function' which we considered in Chapter 4. Both terms refer to the uniquely human ability to reflect upon experience and learn from it, although executive function also refers to the capacities for impulse control and self-management which humans acquire (to varying degrees) as they develop.

TASC aims to help children develop the higher-order skills of metacognition and executive function by encouraging an explicit focus on the process of what we might describe, to use a term from the adult world, as 'project management'. Like many approaches, TASC also stresses the importance of first-hand experience and hands-on learning. This is derived in large part from the influence of Robert J Sternberg and Albert Bandura, two notable American psychologists (Bandura was in fact Canadian but spent most of his career in the USA). The theories of both men are extensive and a great deal of their thinking has been subtly incorporated into the rationale and methodology of TASC. From Sternberg comes the *triarchic* theory of intelligence. This is his model of intelligence comprising *critical*, *creative* and *practical* thinking skills, the third in particular being often overlooked in traditional curricula, according to Sternberg. (You will probably have noticed a similarity between this idea and the *multiple intelligences* model of Howard Gardner, examined in Chapter 4.) Bandura's contribution to TASC includes his ideas about the importance of copying and modelling in children's development. From elements of these theories and from the theories of Vygotsky and others, Belle Wallace and collaborators constructed the TASC model. Each word that the acronym stands for is important: 'Thinking Actively in a Social Context'. A fuller account can be found in books written and edited by Belle Wallace and on the TASC Wheel website.

PRACTICAL TASK PRACTICAL TASK PRACTICAL TASK PRACTICAL TASK PRACTICAL TASK

Next time you introduce a topic in any curriculum area in which you will be focusing on knowledge and understanding – which gives you plenty of choice! – try using a KWL grid. This is a widely-used approach, which is loosely associated with the TASC model. Simply provide the children with a sheet of paper divided into three columns with K, W and L at the top of each column. Before you begin the topic, ask the children to identify what they already know (K) and what they want (W) to find out. Use this information to plan the topic in such a way that at least some of these wishes can be met. Then, at the end, ask the children to list what they have learned (L). With younger children you can write on behalf of the class or a group, or individuals if you have the opportunity. This simple exercise creates great potential for children in forward planning, reviewing, making connections and for that all-important skill: metacognition. An interesting variation on this technique is Stephen Bowkett's What-Do-We-Know-Triangle (Bowkett, 2007, p46)

Edward de Bono's Six Thinking Hats

Another very useful classroom approach which supports the development of children's thinking skills is the Six Thinking Hats devised by a major contributor to thinking skills, Edward de Bono. The Six Thinking Hats is an approach to the development of thinking skills which can help children to think systematically about problems based upon the notion of 'parallel' thinking. De Bono (1993) notes that, without a discipline to direct thinking and attention, the problem solving of both children and adults is often disorganised, with participants moving haphazardly from one mode of thinking to another and wasting a lot of time. The Six Thinking Hats involves participants thinking about a problem systematically using different modes of thinking in parallel and de Bono identifies these modes through the metaphor of the six hats. The whole group 'puts on' each hat in turn and thinks about the problem from that perspective. The modes of thinking signified by the hats are as follows.

- The White Hat is concerned with information. Participants consider the information which will be necessary to tackle the problem.
- The Red Hat is concerned with emotion. While wearing the Red Hat participants acknowledge and express their emotional response to the problem.
- The Yellow and Black Hats are concerned, respectively, with the advantages and disadvantages of the problem and allow optimistic and pessimistic views of the situation to be considered in turn.
- The Green Hat is concerned with creative responses to the problem (and here there is a link with another of de Bono's concepts, that of 'lateral thinking'). Novel, unexpected ideas and solutions are encouraged while the Green Hat is being worn. The mode of thinking signalled by the Green Hat is *creative*.
- The Blue Hat is a little different from the others as it is concerned with managing this process of thinking. In a meeting, the facilitator would wear the Blue Hat to move the process forward, summarising, refocusing and so on as appropriate. The whole group can share this responsibility, even if one individual takes the leading role.

The Six Thinking Hats is a subtle process which requires skill and discipline if it is to be used effectively. You should note that the 'hats' or modes of thinking are not ranked or judged according to their usefulness. Still less are they designed to be assigned to individuals in a fixed way, as can sometimes happen in classrooms. Taking the Yellow and Black Hats as an example, de Bono observes that although people tend to Black Hat (negative, pessimistic) thinking more naturally than they do to Yellow Hat (positive, optimistic) thinking, both are valid and both are important to explore as a solution is sought. Crucially, the whole group will, figuratively, put on a certain hat together and the teacher can direct this, sometimes using just one hat for a particular purpose. The teacher may say, for example, to a group who are familiar with this model: 'OK I'd like us to do some Green Hat thinking about how we can look after our classroom environment,' or 'Let's do some White Hat thinking about all the things we need to find out for our Vikings video'.

The hats are in fact metaphors for different ways of thinking but many teachers find it useful to have illustrations or actual hats of the appropriate colours available to make the process more tangible, especially with younger children. Like the other teaching approaches considered in this chapter, the Six Thinking Hats can be used with children across the primary age range but it needs to be adapted to suit the age and interests of particular groups of children. An approach which resembles the Six Thinking Hats but which can be simpler to introduce is the Plus, Minus and Interesting (PMI) which is explained in the following task.

Another of Edward de Bono's very useful techniques is the PMI. When you have an idea that you want your children to explore creatively, ask them to list their ideas under three headings: Plus (the advantages), Minus (the disadvantages) and Interesting (the ideas which just arise but do not fit into either of the other categories). This can be an excellent device for freeing up creative ideas and ensuring, as with the more elaborate Six Thinking Hats, that ideas are examined systematically and in parallel. Give a fairly brief amount of time for each category to maintain energy and momentum. Considering the idea 'Children should make their own school dinners' for example, children might identify 'independence' and 'choice' among the Plus points, 'losing time to play' and 'making staff lose their jobs' among the Minus points and 'linking up with other schools online to share recipes' as an Interesting point.

The PMI is one of a collection of techniques that Edward de Bono has developed over several decades and which he refers to collectively as the Cognitive Research Trust (CoRT) techniques. There are other powerful tools to stimulate creative thinking too, one example being the use of *random words*, (described in de Bono, 1993). Edward de Bono has written more than 60 books over almost half a century and two particularly useful texts (de Bono, 1985, 1993) are listed on page 88, along with two resource books he has written (de Bono, 1992a, 1992b). Also listed is a website where you can get further information and training in these techniques.

Guy Claxton and Learning Power

Guy Claxton is an important educationalist whose ideas have been mentioned already in this book. He is both a critic of aspects of contemporary schooling (his book *What's the point of school?* (Claxton, 2008) should be on every student teacher's reading list) and an advocate of alternative approaches, based to a large extent on his analysis of what makes an effective learner and his background in psychology. He sums up much of this advice in the phrase *Building Learning Power*, the title of another of his books (Claxton, 2002). Before examining Claxton's ideas about Learning Power a little more thoroughly, I should acknowledge that here and a little later in this chapter I am deliberately fudging the distinction between learning and thinking. I am of course aware that these two processes are different and they have been treated as such throughout this book. However, the neuroscientific perspective now becoming available to teachers (and to which you were introduced in Chapter 4) alerts us to the fact that the distinctions between the two activities are by no means as clear as we once imagined. Whatever uncertainties exist in the picture emerging from neuroscience (and there are many as we have seen), our insights from that field of science to date have raised serious doubts about the view that many people held previously about thinking. That view of thinking might be compared to visiting a library, where books are taken from the shelves, consulted and then returned exactly to their previous location with perhaps an occasional change to the library stock as learning takes place. As we have seen, however, the neuroscientific picture of what happens in our brains when we think is a far more dynamic one and suggests that when we engage in almost any cognitive activity we are in fact learning, as synaptic combinations and pathways in our brains are strengthened or replaced. It is of course possible to conceive of thinking that leaves our neurology unchanged but this seems extremely atypical. Put rather crudely, to a very significant extent when we are thinking, we are also learning. This does not mean that we always learn what is right.

Claxton suggests that *learning power means working on four aspects of students' learning*. These are easily remembered as they all start with the letter 'R': Resilience, Resourcefulness, Reflectiveness and Reciprocity (Claxton, 2002, p17). In taking this perspective, Claxton is offering teachers and learners some profoundly important insights into the learning process. We all know of people (perhaps including ourselves) who may be very intelligent but struggle to maintain their focus when faced with the inevitable setbacks which occur on the learning journey. These people – adults and children – need to develop Resilience. In fact, as Claxton points out elsewhere (Claxton, 2008), it is sometimes the most successful children who struggle most when faced with difficulty. Every child has to recognise that learning is hard and you can model this yourself by admissions that you do not know something and that you and your children are therefore taking a shared journey toward knowledge. This accords with Matthew Lipman's view of the educational enterprise.

Resourcefulness, for Guy Claxton, refers to both practical and cognitive adaptability, a capacity to seek out new possibilities and meanings. It also means *playing with situations* and *being ready, willing and able to learn in different ways* (Claxton, 2002, p17). Claxton's final pair of Rs – Reflectiveness and Reciprocity – echo ideas that many educationalists have developed and which have been referred to throughout this book. The links between Reflectiveness and metacognition should be apparent, as should the links between Reciprocity and collaborative learning, and some further links will be suggested in the final chapter. A word of warning should be sounded here, however. Writers choose their words very carefully and they are generally mindful of other writers' contributions to their own fields. Their words add to rather than simply repeating what has been said already. Take care, therefore, not to assume that Guy Claxton's ideas are exactly the same as those of other thinkers we have considered. There are strong similarities though and his ideas add richness to our picture of thinking and learning.

PRACTICAL TASK PRACTICAL TASK **PRACTICAL TASK** PRACTICAL TASK **PRACTICAL TASK**

What can you do to help children develop the four Rs that Guy Claxton has identified? Is the learning environment in your classroom one which is conducive to Reflectiveness and Reciprocity? Do you commend children for Resilience and Resourcefulness as well as for their more tangible achievements?

Towards a more holistic model

The description of thinking skills that we examined on page 73 is important for you to be aware of when you are planning activities, but it is also important to have a more holistic picture which will give you an idea of what children with these skills will be like. We therefore need to list the attributes of good thinkers as well as types of thinking. This time, instead of asking a question like 'What are thinking skills?' we can ask questions which invite this broader view. Robert Fisher does this when he asks *What is a good thinker?* and he lists 12 *intellectual virtues* gathered into three categories as his own answer to this question (Fisher, 2008, p4). Similarly, Costa and Kallick suggest 16 *Habits of Mind*, a Habit of Mind being *a disposition toward behaving intelligently when confronted with problems, the answers to which are not immediately known: dichotomies, dilemmas, enigmas and uncertainties* (www.education.exeter.ac.uk/projects.php?id=66).

In order to help you to make sense of the approaches that follow as you assess their usefulness for your practice I think it is helpful to pose a similar question: What are the attributes of good thinkers? In response to this question I shall now offer my own list of ten attributes of good thinkers:

1. They are effective problem solvers who can efficiently process all of the information and perspectives relevant to a problem, making sensible judgements about their validity. They are comfortable in their use of abstract representational systems when solving problems and communicating their results.
2. They are able to construct and follow well-reasoned arguments in pursuit of a conclusion but they are also respectful of the arguments put forward by others and are able to revise their views when the arguments of others appear stronger than their own.
3. They work hard to develop their own knowledge, skills and understanding across various areas of learning, bringing a critical but appreciative awareness to each area, and they are able to access the results of their learning efficiently when required.
4. They are aware of their own thinking processes and work to develop these in whatever field they find themselves, reflecting frequently upon their experience and understanding in order to improve these processes.
5. They are capable of independent and creative thought, demonstrating this in their ability to use conventional solutions to problems, to adapt these or to find entirely new or novel solutions as appropriate.
6. They have well-developed interpersonal and communication skills and are attuned to their own emotions and those of others. They understand the balance which must be struck between individual and collective thinking in problem-solving situations.
7. They have the confidence and tenacity to persist in their attempts to solve a problem in the face of adversity, alone or in a group.
8. They are flexible and courageous in their thinking, taking account of their previous experiences, gut feelings and intuitions but not allowing their thinking to be narrowed by premature conclusions or prejudices.
9. They have a sound ethical basis to their thinking, demonstrating care for other people in the larger and smaller communities to which they belong. They have a strong sense of justice which informs their thinking.
10. They have a steadily evolving appreciation of the world that they live in and they act in a principled way to have a positive impact upon it through their actions.

Clearly this list is contestable – a very important idea in philosophy as we have seen. Others considering this issue would almost certainly make different choices to my own and would configure their own lists differently. CJ Simister, for example, offers her own list of 20 dispositions of an *active thinker and learner* (Simister, 2007, p23) which incorporates aspects of the Habits of Mind model and, like my own list, Simister amalgamates learning and thinking. In putting my list together I have deliberately avoided terminology and concepts associated with particular approaches to the teaching of thinking skills, although I have been mindful of these approaches in drawing it up and you can probably see many such links yourself.

Having explored thinking skills in various ways, and acknowledging that debate about their nature can continue indefinitely, I shall conclude by suggesting that the term 'thinking skills' refers to the broad set of cognitive and affective attributes which will help children or young people to lead a productive and fulfilled life within the communities to which they belong.

PRACTICAL TASK PRACTICAL TASK **PRACTICAL TASK** PRACTICAL TASK **PRACTICAL TASK**

Most teachers use their classroom environment to enrich their children's learning. You may therefore have set up walls in your own classroom to support the development of children's reading, creative writing, art, topic work and so on. Try introducing a 'thinking wall' to capture and celebrate children's thinking as it emerges. Also consider giving your children 'thinking books' in which they can record their own thoughts however they wish.

A SUMMARY OF **KEY POINTS**

> Regular sessions based on approaches such as P4C or TASC can help your children to develop thinking skills. These are hard to define precisely but include the skills of enquiry and investigation, the ability to process different forms of information, the ability to communicate effectively and the ability to engage in metacognition.

> There are strong links between P4C and dialogic teaching.

> Approaches such as P4C and TASC also help children to develop the range of skills that we often refer to as 'emotional intelligence'.

> Techniques such as the Six Thinking Hats and PMI designed by Edward de Bono can extend children's thinking skills, particularly in the area of creativity.

> Guy Claxton's ideas about Building Learning Power can help children develop the personal qualities needed to learn (and think) effectively.

> The term 'thinking skills' is problematic and we will probably never be able to define it to everyone's satisfaction. It is important, though, to have a picture of the child who exemplifies these skills as well as the skills themselves.

REFERENCES REFERENCES **REFERENCES** REFERENCES **REFERENCES** REFERENCES

Alexander, R J (2008) *Towards dialogic teaching*. (4th edition) York: Dialogos.

Bowkett, S (2007) *100+ ways for teaching thinking skills.* London: Continuum.

Claxton, G (2002) *Building learning power.* Bristol: TLO.

Claxton, G (2008) *What's the point of school?* Oxford: One World.

Cleghorn, P (2003) *Thinking through philosophy 3.* Blackburn: Educational Printing Services.

de Bono, E (1985) *Six thinking hats.* London: Penguin.

de Bono, E (1992a) *Six thinking hats for schools resource book, Book 1.* Victoria (Aus): Hawker Brownlow Education.

de Bono, E (1992b) *Six thinking hats for schools resource book, Book 2.* Victoria (Aus): Hawker Brownlow Education.

de Bono, E (1993) *Teach your child how to think.* London: Penguin.

DfEE (1999) *The National Curriculum: handbook for primary teachers in England.* London: HMSO.

Fisher, R (1996) *Stories for thinking.* Oxford: Nash Pollock Publishing.

Fisher, R (2008) *Teaching thinking. Philosophical enquiry in the classroom.* (3rd edition) London: Continuum.

Flavell, J H (1976) Metacognitive aspects of problem solving, in Resnick, L B (ed.), *The nature of intelligence.* Hillsdale, NJ: Erlbaum.

Fox, R (2001) Can children be philosophical? *Teaching Thinking*, 4: 46–49.

Hattie, J (2008) *Visible learning. A synthesis of over 800 meta-analyses relating to achievement.* London: Routledge Education.

Lipman, M (2003) *Thinking in education.* (2nd edition) New York: Cambridge University Press.

Matthews, G (1994) *The philosophy of childhood.* Cambridge (Mass.): Harvard University Press.

McCall, C (2009) *Transforming thinking.* Abingdon: Routledge.

Mercer, N (2000) *Words and minds: how we use language to think together.* London: Routledge.

Moseley, D, Baumfield, V, Elliot, J, Gregson, M, Higgins, S, Miller, J and Newton, D P (2005) *Frameworks for thinking. A handbook for teaching and learning.* Cambridge: Cambridge University Press.

Murris, K (2000) Can children do philosophy? *Journal of Philosophy of Education,* 34(2): 261–79.

Murris, K (2001) Are children natural philosophers? *Teaching Thinking,* 5: 46–49.

Richard, E (2005) *10 critical thinking card games.* New York: Scholastic.

Simister, C J (2007) *How to teach thinking and learning skills.* London: Paul Chapman.

Wallace, B (ed) (2002) *Teaching thinking skills across the Early Years.* Abingdon: David Fulton Publishers.

White, D (2001) *Philosophy for kids.* Waco: Prufrock Press.

TV Programme

BBC (1990) *Socrates for six year olds.* From the series *Transformers.*

Useful websites

You can find out more about training, resources and a range of other useful information about P4C, TASC and Edward de Bono's approaches including Six Thinking Hats at www.sapere.org.uk, www.tascwheel.com and www.debonofoundation.co.uk. A very useful website containing resources about P4C is www.p4c.com.

For more information about the ideas and work of Guy Claxton, visit www.guyclaxton.com.

For more information about CoPI visit www.strath.ac.uk/cll/cpd/copi and about Open Spaces for Dialogue and Enquiry (OSDE), visit www.osdemethodology.org.uk/.

The Thinking Skills database Thinking Skills in Primary Classrooms can be found on the DCFS Standards Site at www.standards.dcsf.gov.uk/thinkingskills.

The Cognitive Education Centre contains many useful links and can be accessed at www.education.exeter.ac.uk/projects.php?id=29. The interview with Peter Worley referred to in this chapter can be accessed at www.timlebon.com/blog/labels/philosophy%20in%20schools.html.

7
Talk, thinking and philosophy in the primary curriculum

Chapter objectives

By the end of this chapter you will have considered:

- **ways to encourage the development of talk, thinking and philosophy while teaching across the Areas of Learning in the new primary curriculum;**
- **ways in which reasoning, the use of symbolic systems and many other talking and thinking skills can be developed across the curriculum;**
- **ways to use concept cartoons and puppets while teaching science and other subjects;**
- **adjustments to your regular teaching style which will allow better opportunities for talk and thinking.**

This will help you to make progress towards these Professional Standards for the award of QTS:

Q1, Q4, Q6, Q7a, Q7b, Q8, Q10, Q12, Q14, Q23, Q27, Q28, Q29, Q30, Q32

Introduction

In Chapter 6 we looked at ways in which you could teach thinking skills as a subject in its own right and in this chapter we will look at ways of teaching thinking skills through other subjects. The chapter is organised according to the six Areas of Learning in the new primary curriculum. Sometimes this will require adjusting the ways that you might have been planning to teach in certain areas but the good news is that there will almost certainly be some strategies that you will read about in this chapter that you use already.

There are some important issues to address before we embark upon this second phase. I am sure that by now you will have encountered one of the main sources of frustration facing all teachers and that is the lack of time to cover everything on the curriculum. There is no easy relief from this pressure. However, if we have good subject knowledge and plan carefully we can often find opportunities to 'kill two birds with one stone', dealing with the same skills in different areas of the curriculum. To be able to do this we must understand a little more about what the subjects have in common.

Thinking skills within the primary curriculum

The primary curriculum is certainly diverse but there is a great deal of overlap between the Areas of Learning, particularly in the skills needed by children. These skills are defined by the Essentials for Learning and Life and we examined the scope there for talk, thinking and philosophy in the last chapter. In this chapter we will look at the ways in which these skills can be developed within the subject structure, the six Areas of Learning. Before looking at the Areas of Learning, we will first consider the subjects they contain and the possibilities they offer.

Many subjects offer children opportunities to conjecture and hypothesise, science being the most obvious example. Science is also a subject (or subjects in secondary school) which requires the use of evidence and data but it is by no means the only subject in which these skills are required. They are also essential aspects of history and geography and other subjects too. In fact, it is interesting to notice that the same item might even be used as evidence in different contexts. To take an example, an old Bible could be a piece of historical evidence but it could also be used as a religious artefact in RE and its language style and decoration might be explored in English or art lessons.

Use of artefacts and other examples of 'real' evidence are essential first-hand experiences for children and you should include them in your teaching as often as possible. A study of the local area in history, for example, can be made far more engaging for children if real people are interviewed, real buildings and locations are visited and original documents such as census materials and old photographs are studied. These kinds of experiences help children to gain a sense of how historians (or geographers or scientists) see the world and the particular ways they act within it. They also make it easier to resist the temptation to turn all such enquiries into predominantly literacy activities, such as reading comprehension or poorly focused topic work involving only the recycling of information extracted from books or internet sources. If these last kinds of activities are the only ones you include, your children will miss out on crucial aspects of subjects like history and science. By contrast, other approaches we will consider lead inevitably to a great deal of talking and thinking and they could provide stimuli for philosophical enquiry.

There are some thinking and learning skills which virtually all subjects offer. These include: comparing and contrasting; learning facts, skills and procedures; communicating and colla-borating; decision-making; creating, designing and/or generating ideas; and evaluation. The good news therefore is that for any particular set of skills, careful blending of subjects, or Areas of Learning, from across the curriculum will allow frequent opportunities for their development. Although we must be careful not to overlook the differences between these opportunities, children can gain experience of hypothesising, for example, in subjects as diverse as science and geography.

Many subjects also offer children the opportunity for two areas of thinking that we have not yet considered. These are the use of symbolic systems of various kinds and the use of formal reasoning. We will examine each of these in turn.

Symbolic systems

When children learn how to recognise letters and numbers, then later to use these them-selves, they are developing expertise in two of the most commonly used symbolic systems in our culture. In fact, as an adult trainee teacher with sophisticated skills in these areas, you have probably forgotten how difficult it was to develop these skills and the understanding that accompanied them. But there are other symbolic systems that children encounter in their studies too, such as musical notation, map-symbols, computer languages and the use of any language the child encounters. Occasionally, in subjects like history and RE, children will meet symbols from other cultures and religions, and art often involves the use of symbols and other forms of representation.

Use of any of these symbolic systems may help with the acquisition of others, although there is no guarantee that that will happen (children who struggle with mathematics may excel at language, for example, or vice versa). It is certainly useful for children to reflect on the idea that there are many situations around us where symbols represent or (in more child-friendly language) stand for a variety of things. There is also a connection here with the distinction between literal and metaphorical meaning that comes to children's attention more frequently in literature and art as they get older.

Types of reasoning

Reasoning clearly arises to some degree in most areas of life. When a parent or teacher explains to children that they must put on their wellingtons to avoid getting their feet wet, the adult and the children are involved in a process of reasoning. The children may accept the logic of this argument and do what they have been asked to do or, as every parent knows, they may offer a counter-argument such as 'But my wellingtons hurt my feet' or even 'But I *want* to get my feet wet!' Some curriculum subjects allow children greater opportunities to develop these skills than others. There are, though, two more formal types of reasoning that children will encounter at some point. These are called 'inductive' and 'deductive' reasoning and to a great extent they mirror one another and co-exist within the primary curriculum. Inductive reasoning occurs much more frequently but it is important to understand the relationship between the two.

Inductive reasoning arises when we infer a conclusion from many observations which appear to confirm that conclusion. When young children notice that the sounds that dogs make differ from those that cats make, they are engaging in inductive reasoning which might be articulated along these lines: 'Every dog I have ever heard barks and every cat that I have ever heard miaows. Therefore (I conclude that) dogs cannot miaow and cats cannot bark.' You might notice that there is something a little unsatisfactory about this kind of reasoning since it is possible to at least imagine that a dog might make a sound that is very close to a miaow and a cat to a bark. This is a problem with inductive reasoning which has troubled philosophers, scientists and other thinkers for many centuries. Put simply, we might observe a thousand examples which appear to confirm the same conclusion but we can never be absolutely sure that the next instance will not be a counter-example. Children (or adults) observing elephants in Africa might reasonably conclude that 'all elephants have tusks', not realising that many Asian elephants are tuskless. The conclusion that they have come to would therefore need to be amended. This is always a possibility when we use inductive reasoning.

Deductive reasoning is potentially a source of greater certainty (although you should be aware that the extent to which this is true has been a recurrent cause of disagreement among philosophers). Deductive reasoning arises when we use two statements (philosophers call these propositions), which we call the premises, to lead to a third, which we call, in more ordinary language, the conclusion. A classic form in which deductive reasoning can be expressed is a 'syllogism' and you may have seen this famous example before. (Some philosophers regard it as a little hackneyed but it is a useful example to illustrate the structure of such arguments.)

Example 1:
All men are mortal
Socrates was a man
Therefore Socrates was mortal.

This kind of argument is described as being valid and, for an argument to be valid, the conclusion must follow from the premises. Note, however, that this is not the same as saying that the conclusion is true. The following argument is also valid but it is patently untrue.

> *Example 2:*
> All men are green
> Socrates was a man
> Therefore Socrates was green

Many philosophers distinguish between the two examples above by saying that the argument made in Example 1 is sound, while that made in Example 2 is not because the premises on which Example 2 are based are untrue. You should therefore recognise that for a conclusion of this kind to be true it must have premises (the first two statements) which are true and the conclusion must inescapably, or as philosophers express this, it must necessarily follow from them. We may never use words like 'syllogism' in a primary classroom nor will we analyse arguments in as technical a way as we have done here. However, both you and your children will often find other, more straightforward ways of drawing attention to the logical principles underlying arguments and many children will intuitively work them out for themselves. Indeed, much work in philosophy recently has been concerned with 'informal logic' of this kind.

The subject which allows most scope for deductive reasoning in a formal sense is mathematics although, at primary level, more inductive reasoning is generally to be found. A child's reasoning ability can be built up in many subjects though.

REFLECTIVE TASK

Is this syllogism valid?

> Example 3:
> *All men are mortal*
> *Socrates was mortal*
> *Therefore Socrates was a man*

You probably suspect (rightly) that it is not. Can you imagine a counter-example? You will probably find it easier to use a different name from Socrates to do so (try Alice, for example) and this illustrates how much the context helps us to clarify our reasoning. This is very true for children too. Notice how much more difficult it is for young children to work out 2 + 3 = 5 than it is for them to add two items to another three and work out that there are five. There is far more that could be said about logic and reasoning and there are many comprehensive guides available. A very useful book on thinking skills generally which provides a slightly fuller guide to formal reasoning is Philip Cam's *20 Thinking Tools* (2006).

Subjects and Areas of Learning

Why are the traditional subjects in the primary curriculum being reorganised into Areas of Learning? To answer this question fully would require too great a deviation from our present concerns but it is important for you to understand something about this. (See Smith, 2008 for a more detailed account.) From at least the time of the Plowden Report of 1967 (DES,

1967), the primary curriculum in this country has alternated between a subject-led approach and a thematic approach. The Areas of Learning in the new primary curriculum represent a move towards a thematic approach. The word 'thematic' (other words you will hear include topic-based or context-based) here refers to the way in which traditional subjects like history and science can be taught within themes designed to engage children's interests. This approach is therefore cross-curricular.

It is important for those entering the profession at this time to be aware that, when thematic, cross-curricular approaches have been adopted in the past there have been significant concerns about certain aspects of this approach. Some critics have never been happy about the integration of traditional subjects into a thematic approach. A greater problem, though, is that this approach has, in the past, placed very considerable demands upon the class teacher if it was to be effective. Concerns about the thematic approach taken in the post-Plowden years culminated in a damning, government-initiated report (Alexander *et al.*, 1992) which prompted a return to a more subject-led approach to the primary curriculum. The introduction of the National Literacy and Numeracy Strategies (DfEE, 1998 and 1999b) consolidated this trend and by the late 1990s the primary curriculum was defined by subjects as you can see from the current National Curriculum (DfEE, 1999a). Cross-curricular work was not prohibited within this model and many teachers did maintain it but subjects were the dominant organisational structures.

Since the turn of the millennium, however, the primary curriculum has been moving back towards a thematic approach again. Great emphasis has been placed upon creativity by many practitioners in recent years and many schools operate what they describe as a 'creative curriculum', while attempting to retain the subject rigour which many feel that the years of more subject-driven teaching have produced.

Two major primary reviews in recent years (Alexander, 2009; DCFS, 2009) tried to steer a sensible course in their recommendations about what a new primary curriculum should look like. The two reviews have inevitably sounded some notes of caution since they have been led by Professor Robin Alexander and Sir Jim Rose, two of the authors of the damning report into primary practice mentioned above (Alexander *et al.*, 1992). You will also have noticed Professor Alexander's name many times in this book as the champion of dialogic teaching. The Cambridge Primary Review, led by Professor Alexander (2009), was the more independent and wide ranging of the two and many of its conclusions – including its curriculum model – are innovative and challenging. More emphasis has been placed upon the *Rose Review* (DCSF, 2009) in this book as the curriculum model it proposed was adopted in full as the basis for a new primary curriculum by the Labour government which set it up.

One key element of the new primary curriculum – the Essentials for Learning and Life – was examined in Chapter 6. The other element which is important for this book is the reconfigur-ing of curriculum subjects into six Areas of Learning which will allow them to be combined, where appropriate, within a thematic approach or taught alone. These Areas of Learning are similar, but not identical, to those which define the curriculum of the Foundation Stage and this offers useful continuity for children at the transition point between the two. The skills, knowledge and understanding in each Area are broken down in most cases into three age phases – Early, Middle and Later – which cover the full primary age range from 5 to 11. This allows for even more precise building upon what has happened in the Foundation Stage. In the remainder of this chapter we will focus on each of the six Areas of Learning in the new primary curriculum. Clearly these must be illustrative rather than exhaustive surveys but within each of the Areas of Learning we will examine some of the opportunities for talk, thinking and philosophy and the ways that these can help children reach the learning objectives suggested.

English, communication and languages

Spoken languages – the role of discussion, collaboration and philosophy
This seems a good place to begin as one of the three focal points of this book – talk – is included in this Area although, as we have noted many times already, language and thought occur in every subject. As we have explored talk so much in other chapters, it will be dealt with more briefly here. You can see from its name that this Area also includes the teaching of languages other than English. The usefulness of foreign language learning for the development of children's thinking was mentioned on page 90 when we looked at the use of symbolic representation. In Chapter 6 we considered the ways in which talk and thinking were encouraged in the Essentials for Learning and Life but there is further encouragement for them both in this Area. Under Speaking and Listening, the following objectives are stated under the Programme for upper Key Stage 2 (the part of the Programme labelled 'Later').

> *L1. to convey complex ideas, using different techniques for clarity and effect*
> *L2. to select relevant ideas and use appropriate vocabulary to engage and maintain the interest of listeners*
> *L5. to sustain different roles, deal with disagreement and vary contributions in group discussion*
> *L6. to extend and justify their opinions and ideas, building on what they have heard*
> *L7. to use dialogue and discussion to build up . . . agreement collaboratively*

Clearly all of these would be developed using many of the approaches suggested in this book and they are compatible with the aims of dialogic teaching, collaborative learning and most discussion-based approaches. P4C, TASC and Kagan approaches offer children excellent opportunities to develop in these ways and you should return to Chapters 5 and 6 for further guidance if necessary.

REFLECTIVE TASK

Think back to the approaches to classroom talk suggested in Chapter 5, dialogic teaching in particular. Then look again at the Essentials for Learning and Life described in Chapter 6 and the extracts from the guidance for Speaking and Listening detailed above. Make yourself an action plan to introduce a more dialogic approach to your teaching over the next school term.

Enhancing the teaching of reading
Children's thinking and reading skills can be developed in tandem and you should find that some of the collaborative and discussion-based activities we considered in Chapter 5, such as cloze, sequencing and group prediction, all of which involve talk and thinking, will be of considerable benefit to your children. Another strategy is to ask children to devise questions about a text that you have read together. This is an approach based upon P4C pedagogy and, although you may not be able to steer the discussion that follows in a philosophical direction without further training, you should find that the children's engagement and under-

standing of the text improve as you discuss it. In the TV programme *Socrates for six year olds*, mentioned in Chapter 6 (see page 77), a group of six year olds discuss 'Elfie', one of Matthew Lipman's stories. The children refer explicitly to the words they have read as they try to work out, for example, whether Elfie is a girl. This illustrates quite nicely the way in which texts can not only provide stimuli for philosophical enquiries but, in the process of carrying out those enquiries, a deeper appreciation of the text can be gained.

A useful resource pack called *Storywise* has been produced by two leading P4C practitioners (Murris and Haynes, 2000) and includes details of how a range of children's books might be used as stimuli for philosophical enquiry. Another very useful resource is Sara Stanley's book *But Why?* (2004) which suggests ways in which philosophical enquiries might be handled with children throughout the primary age range, mainly through the use of stories. Many well-known children's books lend themselves very well to this approach, containing as they generally do, ideas and dilemmas which are relevant and engaging to their readers. A few examples are given at the end of this chapter (see page 107) but there are many more that you could use equally well. There are also stories written specifically to provoke philosophical enquiry. Robert Fisher and Paul Cleghorn's books were mentioned in Chapter 6 and the books of Steve Bowkett should also be mentioned here. These are children's books (most suitable at Key Stage 1 and very early Key Stage 2) written and illustrated in exactly the same way as 'ordinary' children's books and can therefore sit among them on your library shelves. A few of these are included in the shortlist of children's books on page 107.

Developing more thoughtful writers

Clearly writing is an essential part of many curriculum areas, not just English, and although you are being encouraged to adopt an approach which is based more on talk than you might otherwise have done, this is not intended to undermine the importance of reading and writing, or literacy as the pair are often called in schools. Generally, writing will be far better if it has been preceded by discussion so that children have the opportunity to air and shape their thoughts. You should also recall the discussion of Vygotsky's ideas in Chapter 3 and the strategy of scaffolding which others have developed in the years since his death. There are many useful ways of scaffolding children's writing across the curriculum, including what are known as 'writing frames' which help children to structure their writing. A writing frame for a historical account, for example, might include sentence openings to help children mould their historical understanding into a form of writing appropriate for this purpose. Clearly an account of a scientific experiment or a piece of persuasive writing would need to be structured very differently. (A very useful guide to such strategies is to be found in David Wray's book in the Learning Matters series (Wray, 2006), which was mentioned in Chapter 5.) There is a need for children to organise and carry out their writing on their own at times but this process can be assisted greatly by preparatory exercises in which key facts and arguments are recalled through collaborative activities. Use the display areas in your classroom for any prompts on flashcards, posters, etc. that emerge as you do this.

Regular review sessions can be very valuable and can allow children and the teacher to be engaged together in the feedback loop which is known as formative assessment and is encouraged by such initiatives as Assessment for Learning (AfL). A major study by Hattie (2008) into the effectiveness of various educational interventions (which was referred to in earlier chapters) found that this kind of involvement by children in the learning process results in significant educational gains. Children can also engage in very useful discussions of one another's work at the drafting stage although you must be confident that they will handle this with sensitivity before presenting them with actual children's work. A useful preparatory step can be for them to look at composite pieces of work that you have constructed yourself.

Mathematical understanding

As we have already seen, mathematics has great potential in helping children develop both their reasoning skills and their use of symbolic representation. Even in their earliest encounters with numbers – when they first learn to count – children are reasoning with abstract ideas. The number five may be attached to many concrete examples – the number of brothers that Sally has, the number of DVDs beneath the television. However, the idea that all of these sets are connected by the number five, a concept that mathematics educators refer to as the 'numerosity' or simply the 'five-ness' of five, is an abstract idea and it is unsurprising that most children need many varied experiences to connect their concrete and abstract understandings. The abstraction within mathematics is of course a barrier to many children (and teachers) and we can make the journey through mathematics much easier for children by offering them as many opportunities as possible to talk about their understandings and to represent mathematical ideas without the standard symbols that they must eventually become familiar with. The use of real contexts is essential in developing children's mathematical thinking. You will find encouragement to take this kind of approach in key documentation like the *National Curriculum* (DfEE, 1999a) and the *Primary Framework for Literacy and Mathematics* (DfES, 2006) but in some other countries, notably Holland, this approach is encouraged even more (Askew, 2003).

PRACTICAL TASK PRACTICAL TASK **PRACTICAL TASK** PRACTICAL TASK **PRACTICAL TASK**

Asking children to discuss the methods they have used to solve problems and to work out calculations is recognised as good practice. If this is done in a mechanistic way, however, perhaps because the teacher feels that it ought to form part of the lesson but is not comfortable managing such interactions, then it can be a dull exercise with little appreciable benefit. If, on the other hand, the teacher recognises the value of providing a forum for the sharing of ideas and uses it to develop understanding of the range of choices which mathematics offers, along with a metacognitive reflection on the strategies used, then far more will be gained. Over the next few mathematics lessons that you teach – a week might be about right – try to find appropriate opportunities to share children's methods within your class if you do not do so already and to enhance this practice if you do. Make sure that you vary the children chosen, that you do not let time drag and that you pursue the mathematical content of what is said. Make sure also that other children are allowed into the discussion. Evaluate the difference this makes to your lessons.

The mathematical Area of Learning in the Early Years Foundation Stage is called 'Problem solving, reasoning and numeracy', making it clear that all three elements belong to the whole. The terms 'problem solving' (in mathematics) and 'using and applying mathematics' are often used interchangeably in key documentation, although each can have a slightly different meaning. Lesley Jones unites the two by describing problem solving *as a way of using and applying mathematics* ... but she goes on to observe that problem solving is *almost invariably reduced to the idea of 'word problems' which, in themselves, are thinly disguised calculations wrapped in words* (Jones, 2003, p87). You should try to avoid this trap if you can. 'Realistic' problems, as the Dutch would describe them, allow children the chance to begin their mathematical thinking in the world as they see it and this allows them to use the mathematics they already know as well as developing new strategies. Sometimes it can be helpful too to set up situations which challenge or test children's ideas. This is known as 'cognitive conflict' and can lead to significant breakthroughs in children's learning (see Swan, 2005).

The need to allow more opportunities for talk and reasoning in mathematics lessons is therefore becoming better understood. The National Strategies have initiated a programme known as 'Developing language and reasoning through guided group work in mathematics', providing carefully selected problems with which children can demonstrate and develop their reasoning through discussion, and another programme which is becoming more well known is Liverpool Local Authority's 'Talking Maths'. There are a range of useful resources and publications which have similar aims, including *Talking maths. Talking languages* (Cotton *et al.*, 1993) which gives useful advice about developing talk within mathematics in multilingual classrooms. This last book is published by the Association of Teachers of Mathematics which produces other very useful resources. Another of its publications, *We can work it out!* (Vickery and Spooner, 2004), contains a range of activities to develop collaborative problem solving in the mathematics classroom. Here is an activity of the kind promoted by the projects and publications we have been examining.

Barrier games

Two children (or two small groups) have identical constructional materials (for example connectable cubes, plastic nets of solid shapes, assorted wooden blocks). One child builds something behind a barrier and then instructs the other child (or group) to build the same thing.

Finally, we considered the opportunities to develop formal reasoning in mathematics lessons earlier in this chapter. These opportunities are more clearly in evidence at more advanced levels of mathematics than at primary school level but primary school mathematics can provide good opportunities for informal reasoning where one assumed fact or set of facts is used to justify a further assertion. Strictly, this is not deductive reasoning but it develops similar ways of thinking, in which conclusions are drawn from justifiable premises. Although there will be more evidence of inductive than deductive reasoning in primary mathematics lessons, the rigour of children's reasoning can develop greatly as a result of these experiences. The following example can generate a wide range of arguments.

Odds and evens

Ask children to investigate odd and even numbers. (Older children could be given an open investigation whereas younger children might need questions or statements to investigate.) Eventually the children should be asked to consider statements, like: 'If you add two odd numbers together, you always get an even number'. Ask them whether they can prove that this must always be so. You can arrange for a variety of mathematical apparatus to be close by but do not direct them to it. Some children will use apparatus, some will use drawings and others will attempt a more formal argument, perhaps using some kind of algebraic reasoning. (A very good account of such an exploration is given in Burton, 1984.)

Scientific and technological understanding

Thinking about science

This Area of Learning includes both science and design and technology and has great potential for the development of talk, thinking and philosophy. Unfortunately, many teachers of primary science (especially at the end of Key Stage 2) feel that they should concentrate on the knowledge which they feel children will need to do well in their end-of-key-stage tests. Certainly there is a great deal of knowledge to be learned while studying science. (You can probably remember trying to commit to memory the periodic table or the life processes at some point.) We only have to remember accounts of great scientific discovery though – the theories of Newton or Einstein, for example – to recognise the fact that thinking was the crucial ingredient in allowing them to happen. Another perspective which underlines the importance of thinking in scientific work is to consider any concept that children encounter, even in primary school, and to ask yourself what your own understanding of that concept is. The following Reflective Task will help you to do this.

REFLECTIVE TASK
REFLECTIVE TASK

Consider any scientific concept which you might teach. What do you understand about gravity, for example, or electrical power? You may find yourself recalling pictures or metaphors that seem to explain these phenomena or you may remember how to make a simple circuit, but do these memories give you an understanding of what electricity or gravity is? For the concept you have chosen write or draw your ideas and then reflect upon them. Do they really address the concept or an indirect application?

We often approach scientific concepts in an indirect way with children, giving them terminology – 'gravity', 'friction', 'up-thrust', etc. – with which situations can be described. Children (and adults) can pass tests by using these terms correctly – perhaps by labelling a diagram – without having any real understanding of the concepts they are describing. Deep understanding of topics like this is very hard to gain. Inevitably we do have to teach some concepts in an indirect way and through metaphor – we typically focus on their effects rather than trying to understand their essence – and some accounts of the essence of such concepts would be too challenging for most primary school children. However, having the opportunity, even occasionally, to consider such ideas directly – including, crucially, expressing their own ideas – can be beneficial and could emerge from a classroom philosophy session.

A variety of stimulus materials to generate discussion of children's ideas have been designed by Stuart Naylor and Brenda Keogh with other collaborators at Millgate House Education (web address given on page 107). One very useful example is the 'concept cartoon' which they have been developing over the last two decades. A concept cartoon is, as the name would suggest, a cartoon designed to provoke discussion and thinking about the concept(s) it addresses and it is an excellent stimulus to consider if you wish to move your practice closer to dialogic teaching. Typically, concept cartoons depict children discussing situations which invite scientific ideas (though concept cartoons have now been developed in other curriculum areas such as English and mathematics) and voicing their opinions, which may or may not be justifiable or accurate. The children using the concept cartoon must discuss these ideas and, in doing so, they will inevitably refine their own.

REFLECTIVE TASK
REFLECTIVE TASK

Here is an example of a concept cartoon. What might the children in your class say about the ideas the children in the cartoon are expressing? What do you think about them?

Figure 7.1 Example of a concept cartoon

(Naylor and Keogh, 2000, p140)

You will recall that, in Chapter 5, we noted that posing statements is a very useful strategy to alternate with asking questions (Askew and Wiliam, 1995). In the above example, therefore, we might have asked questions like 'Would you still be able to see a white cat if you put it into a dark room?' but the concept cartoon offers a way of engaging children's interest in this issue to a much greater degree. Another approach which can lead to similar outcomes is Lyn Dawes' 'Talking Points' (Dawes, 2007).

Another approach developed by Millgate House is the use of puppets in the classroom, again with the intention of stimulating dialogue and discussion (Keogh and Naylor, 2009). Children generally love puppets and, used skilfully, they can be very useful resources. A good way to use them, as recommended by Millgate House, is to have them 'join in' with the lesson by making statements or asking questions that stimulate discussion. Helping the puppet 'to learn' can be an excellent motivator for young children in many curriculum areas.

Talk, thinking and technology
The linking of science and technology in this Area is very useful since the two subjects are closely related. To take an example, learning about the properties of materials is in the domain of science but designing an application which uses those materials is in the domain of technology. This Area of Learning contains many clear links with talk and thinking, directing children to 'observe and explore', 'communicate and model' and 'make systematic evaluations', and it is very important to include opportunities for planning before any project and reflection afterwards. The TASC model, which was explored in Chapter 6 lends itself very well to technological projects. At the idea generation stage, Edward de Bono's Six Thinking Hats approach, also explored in Chapter 6, may be valuable in providing a systematic model for considering all perspectives, including the Green Hat to identify creative possibilities.

ICT

This Area of Learning makes a great deal of reference to ICT which, although it is not itself an Area of Learning, also appears across the new curriculum as one of the Essentials for Learning and Life. Today's primary school children are growing up in a world which is entirely different from previous generations in terms of this technology. Many of these developments are computer related: digital televisions, DVD players and interactive game playing through consoles and the internet being just a few examples. Children see the adults in their homes using the internet to shop, study (and, unfortunately, in some cases for less healthy pursuits). Like everything else in children's lives, there are inequalities of access, and many children will see little computer use of any kind in the home. This issue is often referred to as the 'digital divide' and, although substantial resources have been devoted to its remediation, it is likely to persist as each wave of new technology emerges. Most children, though, will at least see, or will themselves use, some computer-related technologies such as mobile phones.

Talk often happens rather unpredictably during computer use – when groups around a computer negotiate a task or when individuals (or groups) communicate from a distance by voice or text – although much depends on the negotiation of task prior to its use. There is, though, a great deal of opportunity for thinking. As with all of your teaching the quality of your input will have a huge effect on the quality of the outcomes. An important connection here is with the use of computer technology to acquire knowledge and this will be explored in Chapter 8.

Historical, geographical and social understanding

Children's developing sense of time and place

The amalgamation of the three subjects which separate at a later stage into history, geography and citizenship into a single Area of Learning has not been without its critics but there are other practitioners and subject specialists who welcome this move. As one leading curriculum development leader has suggested, *[b]ringing these themes together helps give pupils a more holistic view of the world* (Fry, 2010, p38). This Area is also very suitable for the application of TASC (see also a book on the teaching of history by Belle Wallace (2003) and the Six Thinking Hats).

Where does children's understanding of these issues and perspectives begin? When children are very young, their understanding of historical and geographical issues is, like most other learning, linked very closely to their own experiences. Many classrooms include children whose families have their origins and connections across the world and this is a crucial part of those children's identity which it is good to find opportunities to celebrate. Other children's families will have made major moves within the UK and these accounts are just as important to validate. Children's sense of time and place builds up slowly and a young child will find it hard to know how long ago events took place or how far away places are, relative to one another. Gradually, a firmer sense of both history and geography arises and you can help younger children consolidate this understanding through topics which might draw upon family history and family travel (sensitivity is needed here of course) and by looking at familiar items from the past and present, and from different places, such as toys. A key idea here is comparison and contrast, underpinned by questions of sameness and difference and you can use many approaches to bring this out.

Older children are capable of developing increasingly rich ideas about events in the past and the ability to comprehend these events and, eventually, they are able to ask questions about causal relationships and ethical issues. It is important to note, though, that even very young children will hear and see many stories set in the past, sometimes in a real past and sometimes in an imaginary or mythical past, and these ideas and images form part of their cognitive experience from a young age. Keiran Egan's theories, which we explored in Chapter 4 (see page 35), are useful in helping us understand this process.

CLASSROOM STORY

A very experienced P4C practitioner uses philosophical enquiries to deepen children's understanding of a variety of subjects. Her children were studying Henry VIII and their written work was quite descriptive (demonstrating lower-level thinking in Bloom's terms such as recall). After using this area of history as a stimulus for P4C enquiries, she found that the children's writing had moved to a much higher level, as they evaluated Henry's motives with great insight.

A similar process occurs with geographical understanding. Very young children have little sense of comparative distance. Someone reporting a journey to another town or city will perhaps not make a significantly different impression in the child's mind to someone describing a journey to another country, and even the child's own journeys may be similarly undifferentiated. In fact the speed of air travel and the lack of contact with the world beneath can lead to adults as well as children having some difficulty gaining a sense of distance. It is important to note that, as with every other type of understanding, children will vary enormously. In general, though, you should expect a very gradual development of historical and geographical understanding which countless experiences will help children to consolidate. First-hand experiences are vital for children of all ages. It is all too easy for these subjects to become entirely text based at quite a young age. Of course texts are extremely important but they cannot substitute for experiences like visiting locations which are interesting in historical and/or geographical ways (and here we see the value of linking the two) or handling historical artefacts and making conjectures about those who have used them.

Geographical study also involves the use of maps of various kinds and the symbolism they embody. Certainly children should see these being used from a young age but it is a big step from developing an understanding of the function and value of maps to using them yourself. A common mistake, therefore, is to assume that children will understand the conventions of maps, globes and compass directions when they may not. The following Practical Task might help you to understand how gradually these ideas develop.

PRACTICAL TASK PRACTICAL TASK PRACTICAL TASK PRACTICAL TASK PRACTICAL TASK

Try to negotiate within your school for children from several year groups to draw a map of their route to school (an open instruction is best). You might, for example, arrange for this to be done by children in Years 1, 3 and 5 but so long as there is a spread it does not really matter which year groups you choose. One thing that is likely to strike you on viewing the results is that the younger children will generally draw their maps with front elevations of the streets and buildings they travel along. The 'birds-eye view' does not become established, for most children, for quite some time.

Strategies to develop talk and thinking

A variety of very useful resources have been developed which can be used very effectively to develop thinking skills in this area. In history lessons you can often use the hot-seating and freeze-frame drama techniques which we looked at in Chapter 5 (see page 65) to get children to see the world from another perspective. A very popular approach in historical and geographical settings is the 'mystery' which is similar in organisation to the collaborative mathematical games mentioned earlier in this chapter. A mystery involves a story which children must work out from a set of clues. These will probably include irrelevant information and other 'red herrings' and should be discussed collaboratively. They can be designed to bring out geographical ideas (an unusual location or a journey may feature, for example) or historical ideas (the mystery may be set in the past). In either event children must draw upon their historical and geographical understanding as well as their talk and thinking skills as they search for a solution.

Another useful activity is the Living Graph in which children are presented with a line graph in which the line ascends and descends as it moves across the horizontal axis. The Living Graph is an effective strategy in history for providing a visual overview of the changing nature of an historical event, person or period. Children must then assign elements of a story to the graph. If the graph showed temperature and time, for example, and there was a long period of high temperature, followed by a sudden decrease then an increase before the high temperature was restored, we might tell a story like this: 'Joe was driving home on a cold winter evening when his car broke down. He left his car and walked to the nearest village where he booked into a warm hotel and stayed the night.' Children can be given the story elements or can make up their own. These ideas and many more are contained in some very useful publications (Higgins *et al.*, 2001; Leat, 2001; Leat and Nichols, 1999). The last of these is published by the Geographical Association which has extracts from this and other useful texts on its website. Although they have been designed with a secondary classroom in mind, these ideas are easily adaptable to the primary classroom, certainly at Key Stage 2. The web address of the Geographical Association and a number of other subject associations are given on page 107. These are important points of reference for you in a number of ways, one of which is the access to resources they offer.

Developing ethical sensibilities

Several approaches can come together to help children develop their ethical sensibilities, a broader view of which includes the ability to empathise with others, whether or not they have direct contact with these 'others'. The third strand of the Area of Learning we are considering is citizenship and this subject requires children to develop their understanding of *how identities develop, what we have in common, what makes us different and how we organise ourselves and make decisions within communities* (Essential Knowledge, 1c). There are many points of contact here with the (non-statutory) Religious Education Programme of Learning, which suggests that children: *use empathy, critical thought and reflection to evaluate their learning and how it might apply to their own and others' lives* (Key Skills, 2d).

A further, very useful connection here is with a set of approaches often referred to collectively as the 'Global Dimension', an important element of which is helping children to develop their appreciation of the diversity and interdependence of people, at local, national and global levels, and the framework of ethical obligations which might enable fairer societies to emerge. This perspective also deals with environmental issues, another vital area contained within this Area of Learning. Study of environmental issues does not belong exclusively to this Area, however – you can probably think of other Areas of Learning and Essentials for Learning and Life that this would involve.

Returning to the suggestion that we should try to help children develop their awareness of sameness and difference between people, which was made a little earlier, you will probably appreciate that this is not altogether easy since it can lead children into damaging stereotypes when they consider people from different cultural and ethnic backgrounds, whether from this country or overseas. There are many organisations which can give you ideas and resources to deal positively with these issues (some website addresses are on page 107) and you will see that talk and thinking figure prominently in classroom strategies. There are clear links here too with other important initiatives such as Every Child Matters.

As we have seen, P4C can play a very important role, in developing both children's thinking skills and their emotional and interpersonal skills, and this can be applied to the kinds of issues considered here. In secondary schools, practitioners often use P4C in the teaching of Religious Education and related subjects.

Understanding the arts

This Area of Learning involves art and design and music and also includes drama and dance. Clearly, this Area gives enormous richness to the curriculum, allowing children scope for self-expression and creativity regardless of its potential for the development of talk and thinking. There are, though, a number of ways in which the Area can also give rise to the latter.

Interpreting meaning

Words which appear repeatedly in curriculum descriptions in this Area include: 'communication', 'evaluation', 'interpretation' and 'meaning'. Although we must be careful not to be too definitive here, it seems reasonable to suggest that artists communicate – or attempt to communicate – in whatever media they work in. Their communication may simply be the representation of what they see or it may carry some additional message. The role of the viewer is crucial too and, as well as simply enjoying a piece of art, the viewer will look for meanings, including some that the artist may not have been aware of. When we look at the late paintings of Van Gogh for example, it is often suggested that we might see, in addition to his staggering talent, signs of the mental collapse which would lead to his early death. No one suggests that Van Gogh intended to include these signs in his work (if indeed they are there) but the viewer may interpret his work in this way.

All children (and adults) are artists, though the realisation of their potential will vary, and these issues apply to their own work as much as to the work of more famous artists. Children can discuss their own work as well as famous works of art. A useful question to ask children during or after their work is 'What were you thinking/feeling when you drew/painted this?' rather than the more commonly asked question: 'What have you drawn?' You should be careful, though, that interpretation and intellectual analysis of children's art does not detract from the sheer pleasure that can be gained from producing and enjoying art.

Art and music can provide excellent stimuli for philosophical discussions. As well as paintings that might excite a strong reaction (*The Scream* by Munch, *Guernica* by Picasso, the artwork of M C Escher, etc.), you could use other forms of art (the sculptures and installations of Antony Gormley, for example) and you should make sure that you include work by female artists and artists from different cultural and ethnic backgrounds.

We briefly considered three different branches of philosophy in Chapter 6 – metaphysics, epistemology and ethics. In many textbooks, you will find that these three and one more are described as the main branches of philosophy, the fourth being aesthetics. Aesthetics is the study of what we consider to be beautiful and leads to many interesting questions: 'Who decides what is beautiful?', 'Is beauty really in the eye of the beholder?', 'Are standards of beauty fixed or can they change over time?' and so on. Children are generally very interested in these kinds of questions (as the timeless popularity of stories like 'Beauty and the Beast' and 'The Hunchback of Notre Dame' might suggest) and they will often raise remarkably mature questions in philosophical discussions.

The symbolism of music

Involvement with music requires children to listen attentively and, even if they may not realise it, it requires them to engage with patterns and symbols. As with art, it is the combination of elements which creates particular effects. When making or listening to music, children will often have to attend to rhythm and beat – although they will also explore sounds through improvised free time music – and to the blending of sound against a back-drop of silence. Simply by singing they learn about melody, harmony and many other musical elements. If they engage in conventional music by learning to play an instrument, they will also have to learn about pitch and scales and probably, at some point, the symbo-lism of musical notation. There are different types of musical notation. Graphical notation in particular is based around pictorial or graphic symbols to represent the sound in a way which is much more indistinct and open to interpretation than conventional notation and is not necessarily based on rhythm and beat.

Finding different means of expression

While teaching in these areas, your heart will probably have sunk on many occasions already when you have heard your children say 'I can't paint (or draw or sing).' Clearly one response, whether we verbalise this or not, is to try and rebuild the child's artistic confidence through varied activities, but it is a sad reality that there will be children who will struggle with any particular medium we offer so it is important to offer as varied a range of opportunities as possible.

We cannot dwell on the more physical areas of the curriculum such as physical education (included in the final Area of Learning) or dance in this book but it is important to point out that these are vital areas of the curriculum and the primary curriculum would be seriously deficient without them. You should remember, too, from Chapter 4, the broadening of our understanding of children's accomplishments which Howard Gardner's 'multiple intelli-gences' model has given us. It is also important to recognise that physical activities are linked to children's cognitions and emotions and they offer valuable opportunities for evalua-tion and refinement as curriculum guidance suggests.

Advances in technology have opened up newer means of expression to children, such as digital photography and digital video-making. These are far cheaper and easier to process and share than the analogue forms which preceded them. 'Visual literacy' as it is sometimes called, can emerge from such experiences and there can be powerful connections for children between using images of these kinds themselves and reflecting on images used by others. Photographs can be very important stimuli for philosophical enquiry and for other talking and thinking activities.

PRACTICAL TASK PRACTICAL TASK PRACTICAL TASK PRACTICAL TASK PRACTICAL TASK

Give children a set of photographs or reproduction paintings which are connected in some way by a theme and ask them to sort and group them. You might look at photographs which include urban and rural environments for example, or contrasts in wealth. There might be photographs of different textures or paintings of people. Make sure that you do not 'steer' the children in any particular direction. How do they group them? What sort of connections do they make? This activity can be used in a wide range of curriculum areas and could, for example, be an initial stimulus for a historical or environmental study.

Understanding physical development, health and wellbeing

This final Area of Learning is another composite, drawing together physical education and personal, social and health education (this area has been labelled differently at different times and is best known by acronyms like PHSE) and economic education. Physical education and other physical elements within the curriculum were mentioned briefly at the end of the previous section but this Area of Learning also includes the aim of keeping children healthy and safe in many different ways. These include diet and personal hygiene as well as sex and drug education, as far as it is appropriate to teach these in the primary school. Approaches like P4C have a great deal to offer here as we learned when we examined its caring dimension in Chapter 6. The development of critical thinking in the context of children's lives and the decisions they must eventually make, along with a commitment to working in caring and collaborative ways, are central aims of P4C and the regular practice of P4C through the community of enquiry would be highly beneficial in terms of this Area of Learning. There are links again with citizenship (part of historical, geographical and social understanding as we saw earlier) and Religious Education.

One of the key skills in this Area which is identified in the Programme of Learning is: *find information and check its accuracy including the different ways issues are presented by different viewpoints and media* (Key Skills, 2d). From what you have learned so far in this book it should be clear that a philosophical approach can help children to question the basis of truth claims, and when they do so they are engaged in epistemology, the philosophical area we have come across several times already. Try this Practical Task, based on a P4C activity designed by Karin Murris, with your children. You may need to adjust it to take account of their age and experience of this kind of work but you should find the outcome interesting.

PRACTICAL TASK PRACTICAL TASK PRACTICAL TASK PRACTICAL TASK PRACTICAL TASK

Put two columns onto your black/whiteboard, headed 'Things I know' and 'Things I believe'. Ask children to put statements in each column and consider them as a class. Ask the children why they classed particular statements as knowledge or belief. How do they justify their decisions about where their statements should go? Are there any possible grounds for doubting any of the things 'known'? How can we be certain of something? What is a reliable source of evidence?

The level of proof we are prepared to accept varies from situation to situation. As adults, we tend to believe someone who tells us something unless we have reason to doubt their trustworthiness or we think they may be mistaken, but we are probably more sceptical than children about what we hear in the media. Lawyers and police officers are often inclined to seek higher levels of proof before accepting someone's word. Philosophers will often go beyond this point, questioning what most people would take for granted. We will return to epistemological issues in the next chapter.

A SUMMARY OF **KEY POINTS**

> **Talk, thinking and philosophy are extremely important elements to include in your teaching of the new primary curriculum and they relate to all of the Areas of Learning.**

> **Many subjects offer opportunities for: comparing and contrasting; learning facts, skills and procedures; communicating and collaborating; decision-making; creating, designing and/or generating ideas; and evaluation.**

> **Many subjects also offer children the opportunity for the use of symbolic systems and the use of formal reasoning.**

REFERENCES REFERENCES **REFERENCES** REFERENCES REFERENCES REFERENCES

Alexander, R J (ed) (2009) *Children, their world, their education. Final report and recommendations of the Cambridge Primary Review*. London: Routledge.

Alexander, R J, Rose, J and Woodhead, C (1992). *Curriculum organisation and classroom practice in primary schools: a discussion paper*. London: DES.

Askew, M (2003) Word problems: Cinderellas or wicked witches?, in Thompson, I (ed) *Enhancing primary mathematics teaching*. Maidenhead: Open University Press.

Askew, M and Wiliam, D (1995) *Recent research in mathematics education 5–16*. London: HMSO/OFSTED.

Burton, L (1984) *Thinking things through*. Oxford: Basil Blackwell.

Cam, P (2006) *20 thinking tools*. Victoria (Aus): Acer Press.

Cotton, A, Cox, L, Cunningham, R, Gammon, A, Lawlor, G, O'Connor, P, Penfield, C, Preblle, S and Rahman, M (1993) *Talking Maths. Talking Languages*. Derby: Association of Teachers of Mathematics.

Dawes, L (2007) *The essential speaking and listening. Talk for learning at Key Stage 2*. London: Routledge.

DCSF (2009) *Independent Review of the Primary Curriculum: Final Report. (The Rose Report)* Nottingham: DCFS.

DES (1967) *Children and their primary schools*. London: HMSO.

DfEE (1998) *The National Literacy Strategy*. London: DfEE.

DfEE (1999a) *The National Curriculum: handbook for primary teachers in England*. London: HMSO.

DfEE (1999b) *The National Numeracy Strategy*. London: DfEE.

DfES (2006) *The primary framework for literacy and mathematics*. Norwich: DfES.

Fry, C (2010) The global view. *TES Magazine*, 22 January, pp. 37–39.

Hattie, J (2008) *Visible learning. A synthesis of over 800 meta-analyses relating to achievement*. London: Routledge Education.

Higgins, S, Baumfield, V and Leat, D (2001) *Thinking through primary teaching*. London: Chris Kington Publishing.

Jones, L (2003) The problem with problem solving, in Thompson, I (ed) *Enhancing primary mathematics teaching*. Maidenhead: Open University Press.

Keogh, B and Naylor, S (2009) Puppets count. *Mathematics Teaching*, 213. Derby: Association of Teachers of Mathematics.

Leat, D (2001) *Thinking through geography*. London: Chris Kington Publishing.

Leat, D and Nichols, A (1999) *Theory into practice. Mysteries make you think.* Sheffield: The Geographical Association.

Murris, K and Haynes, J (2000) *Storywise: thinking through picture books.* Newport, Pembrokeshire: Dialogueworks.

Naylor, S and Keogh, B (2000) *Concept cartoons in science education*. Sandbach: Millgate House Publishers.

Smith, J (2008) Reconciling subjects and contexts: the case for a pragmatic primary curriculum. *Educational Futures. Journal of the British Education Studies Association Conference Edition,* 1(2): 63–74. Accessible at www.educationstudies.org.uk/

Stanley, S and Bowkett, S (2004) *But why? Developing philosophical thinking in the classroom.* Stafford: Network Educational Press.

Swan, M (2005) *Improving learning in mathematics: challenges and strategies.* DfES Standards Unit. Downloadable from www.ncetm.org.uk/resources/1442.

Vickery, A and Spooner, M (2004) *We can work it out! Collaborative problem solving for the mathematics classroom.* Derby: Association of Teachers of Mathematics.

Wallace, B (ed) (2003) *Using history to develop thinking skills at Key Stage 2.* London: David Fulton Publishers.

Wray, D (2006) *Teaching literacy across the primary curriculum*. Exeter: Learning Matters.

Children's books

Bowkett, S (2004) *If I were a spider*. Stafford: Network Educational Press.

Bowkett, S (2004) *Philosophy Bear and the big sky.* Stafford: Network Educational Press.

Browne, A (2008) *Willy the wimp*. London: Walker Books.

Burningham, J (1999) *Would you rather...* London: Random House.

Inkpen, M (1995) *Nothing.* London: Hodder Children's Books.

Foreman, M (1974) *Dinosaurs and all that rubbish*. London: Puffin Books.

McKee, D (1983) *Tusk Tusk.* London: Sparrow Books.

Sendak, M (1967) *Where the wild things are.* London: The Bodley Head.

Useful websites

Subject association and subject-based websites include:

www.nate.org.uk (English); www.ncetm.org.uk and www.atm.org.uk (both mathematics); www.ase.org.uk and www.sciencelearningcentres.org.uk (both science); www.history.org.uk; www.geography.org.uk; www.nsead.org (art and design).

Global Dimension information can be obtained from www.dea.org.uk; www.dep.org.uk; www.oxfam.org.uk/education/gc and other sources.

Other useful websites include www.millgatehouse.co.uk and www.dialogueworks.co.uk.

8
Developing a Thinking School

Chapter objectives

By the end of this chapter you will have considered:

- **ways to encourage the development of talk, thinking and philosophy across the primary school.**

This will help you to make progress towards these Professional Standards for the award of QTS:
Q1, Q2, Q4, Q5, Q6, Q8, Q10, Q12, Q18, Q24, Q30, Q31

Introduction

This final chapter requires you to step through the door of your own classroom and consider how you might encourage the development of talk, thinking and philosophy across the whole school. A useful name for such a school is a 'Thinking School' and many schools have already adopted this title as a major part of their identity. This chapter will give you ideas for the future if you are still undertaking your initial training. If you are already a more experienced teacher or school leader, you may be able to implement some of these ideas straight away. In the philosophical spirit of this book, it should be noted that others may well offer a different set of recommendations but those offered here draw together the issues raised in previous chapters. We will therefore consider strategies under seven interrelated headings to help a school move towards the goal of being a Thinking School, in the broad sense of thinking developed throughout this book.

A Thinking School is a caring community

You have probably heard the famous African saying 'It takes a village to bring up a child'. This saying expresses very neatly the difficulty of bringing up children within our large, complex and fragmented societies, in contrast to the close-knit community of a traditional village. The saying also reminds us how much effort, expertise and energy must be invested in the upbringing of a child. This investment is essential if children are to have the start in life that they deserve and if accidents of birth are not to determine their futures. In comparing our own society to an abstract picture of a village we must of course take care not to stereotype either of these. Difficulties can still arise in close-knit, highly regulated communities like villages and children can, and do, flourish in the midst of conflicting ideas and lifestyles. (In fact, as we have seen in this book, cognitive conflict is a healthy and natural part of the development of thinking.) The African saying is popular, though, because we recognise a fundamental truth within it. A word which expresses what the best villages have is 'community' and there are some features of a community which are extremely relevant to the development of the Thinking School. One is that, even though there may be disputes, there are common values. Another is that a community offers those within it a sense of belonging and the security that that carries with it. You will recall how important it is to meet needs like this if we are to pave the way for effective thinking and learning and they are therefore prerequisites for the Thinking School.

Schools can be warm, inclusive communities, drawing children and staff together in shared endeavour but not all schools manage this as well as the best. Recent research carried out for the Cambridge Primary Review (Robinson and Fielding, 2007) has suggested that children are generally happy in primary school but that this tends to diminish as they get older. Writers such as Guy Claxton have observed that many young people become alarmingly stress-ridden and disaffected as they move through the school system (Claxton, 2008). It is too easy to jump to the rather complacent conclusion that all is rosy in primary schools and that any problems in the school system lie in the secondary sector. Children learn a great deal in their primary years which affects their progress through secondary schools and into their adult lives beyond. The onerous testing system, which often leads to unnecessary pressures on children and to a distorted curriculum, begins in the primary sector. Additionally, many children leave primary school without the skills they need to cope with the challenges ahead. As well as more academic skills, such as their abilities to speak and listen, to read and write, and to work mathematically, children need to learn the kind of personal skills we have referred to in this book, the skills needed to learn and to live well. In a Thinking School, children will be more able to develop these qualities which will help them to thrive in secondary school and beyond. As we saw in Chapter 6, Guy Claxton's Learning Power model identifies these qualities through four Rs. These correspond quite closely to the four core values within P4C, which are described as the 'Four Cs', and the links are shown below.

Reflectiveness	Critical thinking
Resourcefulness	Creative thinking
Resilience	Caring thinking
Reciprocity	Collaborative thinking
(Claxton, 2002)	(Sapere, 2010)

No single approach to classroom teaching will work in every situation, as we have noted throughout this book, but there is encouraging evidence, from schools that have adopted Claxton's Learning Power model, P4C or other approaches considered in previous chapters, that these have helped children to develop the kind of skills we are considering here. P4C offers a particularly rich pedagogy for teachers and children to develop across the school.

Another vital issue on the road to the Thinking School is to ensure that the governance of your school which is visible to the children is transparently fair. It is no use having classroom practices like P4C, which are based on honesty, fairness and consideration for others, if the way in which school is run outside the classroom is perceived as unfair. This does not mean of course that no child (or adult) will ever be disgruntled about the treatment they receive in school but all school systems should be based on clearly equitable rules and procedures and all staff should be encouraged to adopt as kind and fair an approach as possible in their dealings with children. Many staff do this as a matter of course, and Standard Q1 makes this requirement for teachers explicit, but the pressures of school life can grind down even the most good-willed teacher so encouragement to act in kindly ways are always useful (MacGrath, 2000).

'Pupil voice' was mentioned in Chapter 2. The trend towards allowing pupil voice to be heard wherever it reasonably can be heard, in matters of school governance and learning, has been gathering momentum over a number of years. Structures to channel this now exist in most schools. It is, however, much harder to ensure that this pupil voice has real effects when justifiable, but perhaps controversial, actions are recommended. These are the situations that children will look at with most interest as they assess the extent to which the adults running the school take pupil voice seriously. Edward de Bono's Six Thinking Hats might be a good model to introduce children's representative groups to in order to develop their problem-solving skills.

A Thinking School is a community which celebrates thinking and learning

A Thinking School is one in which learning of any kind, and by anyone, is encouraged and celebrated. Children learn what they see those around them doing, much more than they learn from being told what to do. If they see that their teachers love thinking and learning, they are more likely to pick up the habit themselves so teachers should be encouraged to share their learning passions with children. Following Howard Gardner's *multiple intelligences* model, we should take a broad view of the learning we celebrate. Whether or not Gardner is right to use the word 'intelligence' to describe such a diverse range of human accomplishments, there is no doubt that his ideas can lead to a recognition of talent that might otherwise be marginalised. School assemblies can be an excellent vehicle for this kind of celebration and can involve the wider community of adults as well as children in school. We should also encourage the development of emotional intelligence (Goleman, 1996). As with the term 'multiple intelligences', we can contest the use of the word 'intelligence' here. There seems no doubt, however, that Goleman and others have identified an invaluable cluster of social skills which can smooth a child's journey through a wide variety of settings and these skills should be nurtured in school. The links with the caring aspect of P4C and Claxton's *resilience* should be apparent and both approaches can help children develop these skills. The skills and accomplishments described in this paragraph can be developed within the confines of a particular classroom but the structures of the school, if used well, can magnify their effects.

A Thinking School is one in which connections are encouraged

We have repeatedly noted the importance of children making connections for themselves and of their teachers and other adults helping them to do this. At a neurological level, you will recall that connections are literally being made constantly through the process of synaptogenesis. At the macro-level of the classroom this seems to be linked to the making of cognitive connections or, in less technical language, joining up ideas. The more that we can encourage teachers to help children make connections between different ideas, therefore, the better thinking and learning are likely to take place. Good use of plenary sessions in lessons – both at the end and at key points along the way – should be encouraged across the school and both teachers and children can record their ideas in a wide variety of ways. Mind maps, devised by Tony Buzan (for example, Buzan, 2003), are one useful way of recording ideas and this model is based upon the establishing of connections.

Metacognition is a process that we have considered a great deal in this book and, as we have seen, it is closely linked with another collection of cognitive capacities known as 'executive function'. This set of high-level cognitive skills allows us to organise and plan our thoughts and actions, to control our impulses and to delay gratification where necessary, all of which combine to allow highly effective functioning in most fields. While we do not know precisely how to train children to develop metacognition and executive function, the opportunity to practise these skills in the controlled setting of the classroom seems to lead to their development. Many of the approaches we have considered encourage these skills, the TASC model and P4C being particularly useful in this respect.

A Thinking School is one in which approaches to talk, thinking and philosophy are blended in the best way for its children

It has been suggested at various points in this book that, in order to develop your practice, you should seek further training. Inevitably, training by an expert can be rather expensive for a trainee teacher and so, if you are still engaged in your initial period of training, you may wish to postpone such plans until you have taken up a post in school. If you are now in a position which gives you influence over your school's professional development programme, you are strongly advised to consider setting up whole-school training in one or more of the approaches considered in this book. This is a very useful step towards becoming a Thinking School as it is the best way to ensure that the whole school takes an approach on board and the benefits of this consistency for children are likely to be huge. Taking this deeper approach also helps avoid what John White has described very well as the 'shrink-wrapping' of ideas, where ideas arrive in schools, often second-hand and in an oversimplified form, to be acted upon by busy teachers (White, 2005). Remember that good teachers take responsibility for their own training needs and discuss them with their collea-gues in order to develop their skills and understanding to the highest level for the benefit of the children they teach. The approaches to talk, thinking and philosophy explored in this book work extremely well in combination with one another but the distinctive features of each approach must be recognised and maintained, like the ingredients in a salad rather than those in a soup. Here are two stories of schools which have very successfully blended approaches which encourage talk, thinking and philosophy.

SCHOOL STORY 1

A primary school in a socio-economically deprived urban area had very significant behaviour and attendance problems until staff introduced an innovative curriculum based on a number of thinking skills approaches, including TASC, multiple intelligences and Edward de Bono's Six Thinking Hats. Behaviour, attendance and children's motivation have improved dramatically and the school now achieves some of the best value-added results in the country.

SCHOOL STORY 2

Another very large, multicultural primary school had problems with behaviour. Since the Kagan approach was introduced across the school, both learning and behaviour have improved very significantly. Particularly noticeable is that the gap between high and low achieving children has narrowed. Although the Kagan approach is the main one used in the school, the use of P4C, Guy Claxton's Learning Power and, as in School 1, an innovative curriculum model have each played a part in these improvements.

A Thinking School is one in which questioning is encouraged

A Thinking School should be one in which all claims to knowledge could be questioned. One of the key debates in primary education in the last few years has been between those advocating the teaching of knowledge and those advocating the teaching of skills. As we noted in Chapter 7, the *Cambridge Primary Review* (Alexander, 2009a) was taking findings and making recommendations over roughly the same period of time as the *Rose Review*. Like the *Rose Review*, the *Cambridge Primary Review* makes clear that it is not recommending an entirely skills-based curriculum in which knowledge is seen as arbitrary. A primary head's letter to the *Times Educational Supplement* was quoted in its Interim Report:

> *Children do not need to know lots of dates. They can look up information on Google and store it on their mobile phones.*
>
> (Alexander, 2009b, p15)

This position is given short shrift by the authors of the *Cambridge Primary Review* who respond that

> *[t]o tell children, at the start of lives in which they will be assailed by information that they will fail to evaluate at their peril...that Google and a mobile phone will do the trick, is a travesty of what knowing and understanding ought to be about.*
>
> (Alexander, 2009b, p16)

With all of the changes that we have already seen in our society, there are many who would argue that there are no bodies of information that are any longer sacrosanct and what children need is the skill to find knowledge. (A sophisticated and nuanced variation of this argument is made by Guy Claxton (2008)). It seems unlikely that we will reach the point where no areas of knowledge are thought worthy of learning but two important points seem to be emerging.

1. There may in future be fewer universally desirable bodies of knowledge than at present. Even today, bodies of knowledge that we sometimes think are of universal importance are largely of interest to particular groups and are strongly contested by others – some areas of historical knowledge being a good example.
2. Children will need the skills to find information which purports to be knowledge but, especially with the ever-greater availability of electronic and web-based sources, there will be an even greater need to develop judgement in assessing the validity of these sources (a point usefully developed in November, 2001).

A philosophical approach of the kind developed in P4C would help children develop the skills they require to assess the contestability (as in 1.) and the validity (as in 2.) of the 'facts' they encounter.

A Thinking School would encourage children to personalise their own learning

While the justification offered for personalised learning is sound, there has been some confusion about what it should look like in reality. Some policymakers appear to imagine that class teachers can somehow produce and deliver individualised programmes of work for however many children they have in their class. This would clearly be an impossible demand. If we want to create personalised learning, then, what options are open to us? The approaches considered in this book, which are designed to develop talk, thinking and philosophy, can take us a long way towards the goal of personalised learning. They can do so because they develop autonomy in the children who are taught in this way and this leads to them taking control of their own learning in other areas too (Wilmot, 2006). The Thinking School therefore aims to foster this autonomy and teachers delight in seeing their children managing their own learning. David Hargreaves' 'gateways' to personalising learning (see Alexander, 2009a, pp 304–5) offer a very useful structure which is compatible with many ideas in this book.

Thinking School is a place where dialogue is encouraged

One of the aims of this book has been to encourage you to engage in, as Robin Alexander puts it, *rethinking classroom talk* (Alexander, 2008, subtitle). Two other aims have been to persuade you that talk and thinking are virtually inseparable and that a variety of approaches, in particular the philosophical approach of P4C, can simultaneously develop talk, thinking and a range of caring qualities within the classroom. These aims are intended to develop a better balance between oracy and literacy so that all children can develop the spoken language they need to express their ideas, reasons and emotions (Smith, 2010) as they pass through the vital years of their primary education..

A SUMMARY OF **KEY POINTS**

> **This chapter has considered some of the features which might mark out a Thinking School and how a primary school might move in that direction but, if that is beyond your reach at present, I hope that as a first step you will succeed in creating a Thinking Classroom for you and your children.**

REFERENCES REFERENCES **REFERENCES** REFERENCES **REFERENCES** REFERENCES

Alexander, R J (2008) *Towards dialogic teaching*. (4th edition) York: Dialogos.

Alexander, R J (ed) (2009a) *Children, their world, their education. Final report and recommendations of the Cambridge Primary Review*. London: Routledge.

Alexander, R J (2009b) *Towards a new primary curriculum: a report from the Cambridge Primary Review. Part 2: the future*. Cambridge: University of Cambridge Faculty of Education.

Buzan, T (2003) *Mind maps for kids. An introduction – the shortcut to success at school*. Thorsons.

Claxton, G (2002) *Building learning power*. Bristol: TLO.

Claxton, G (2008) *What's the point of school? Rediscovering the heat of education*. Oxford: One World Publications.

Goleman, D (1996) *Emotional intelligence. Why it can matter more than IQ*. London: Bloomsbury.

MacGrath, M (2000) *The art of peaceful teaching in the primary school*. London: David Fulton Publishers.

November, A (2001) *Empowering students with technology*. Glenview, Illinois: Pearson Skylight.

Robinson, C and Fielding, M (2007) *Children and their primary schools: pupils' voices* (Primary Review Research Survey 5/3), Cambridge: University of Cambridge Faculty of Education.

Sapere (2010) *Philosophy for Children Level 1 course handbook*. (2nd edition). Oxford: Sapere.

Smith, J (2010) Speaking Up: Towards a more oracy-based classroom. *English Drama Media*, 16:

29–33. NATE: Sheffield.

White, J (2005) Howard Gardner: The myth of multiple intelligences. *Viewpoint*, 16. Institute of Education, University of London.

Wilmot, E (2006) *Personalising learning in the primary school.* Carmarthen: Crown House Publishing Ltd.

Useful websites

Information about the (Cambridge) Primary Review (led by Professor Robin Alexander) can be accessed at www.primaryreview.org.uk/ The Final Report is detailed under Alexander, 2009a above.

Support for whole-school development using one of the approaches featured in this book can be obtained from the organisations listed at the end of Chapters 5 and 6

The author, John Smith, has a website which you can access at: www.talkandreason.co.uk

Index